THE MANUAL

A Guide to the Ultimate Study Method (USM)

THE MANUAL

A Guide to the Ultimate Study Method (USM)

•Concentration •Speed Reading •Super Memory •Note Taking •USM
•Rapid Mental Arithmetic

By Rod Bremer

Fons Sapientiae Publishing

Published in the United Kingdom by Fons Sapientiae Publishing, Cambridge, United Kingdom

ISBN 978-0-9569907-0-9

Disclaimer

This book is not intended to replace the services of a trained health professional. All matters and circumstances regarding your health require medical supervision and attention. You are responsible for consulting your physician before adopting the procedures and techniques presented in this book. Any applications of the ideas, techniques and procedures set in this book are at the reader's discretion.

The author and publisher of this material are <u>not responsible</u> in any way whatsoever for any liability, loss, injury or risk, personal or otherwise, which may occur, directly or indirectly, due to reading or following the instructions in this manual.

To my family

Table of Contents

Introduction

There is a profusion of books written about topics related to faster forms of learning and techniques for greater utilisation of the mind; as with everything in life, some are good whilst others make grandiose promises that fail to materialise. The aim of this manual is to provide the reader with the best techniques that achieve the desired goal with the least effort in the shortest time. The approach taken here is unique; the techniques provided are combined into a learning system whose main goal is the practical implementation of thousands of years of research into the human psyche.

The study system presented here is the culmination of the author's 25 years of experimentation with all the latest research, scientific and anecdotal, on the topics of super memory, speed reading, concentration, states of mind, rapid arithmetic and note taking. The author has kept the techniques that work, modified those that were not practical and discarded those that did not provide measurable results. The end outcome is a system that would allow the reader, if he chooses to persevere with the training schedule, to master an approach that would ensure a life time of enjoyable learning experience as opposed to the drudgery of rote learning and cramming. In addition, the ability to perform monumental feats of mind (like memorising a pack of cards in 2 minutes or finding the cube root of 912,673 in 4 seconds) would make one realise how limited our experience of life has been before and how these and other limits we set ourselves are just an illusion that can easily be dispelled.

The manual has been written in the order in which it should be read; the reader is strongly advised to follow the book's instructions since earlier techniques are used in later ones. For example, in order to multiply 7615234 x 9854787 one needs to be able to memorise the result, which is a 14 digit number; without having learnt the memory techniques presented in part 2 it would be impossible to perform the calculation.

Contrary to other well marketed products out there, the author chooses not to make extravagant claims of abilities such as: to be able to read a book in mere minutes or to memorise something once and forever retain it. Instead the exposition of this manual provides the reader with the techniques that work and the training schedule that needs to be undertaken in order to see measurable progress. We provide documented and verified feats achieved by other humans to allow you to perceive what is possible with perseverance and dedication. The important point here is that your motivation should determine how much you time invest, for example, if you never intend to compete in the memory championships or to play professional poker then card memorisation should not be high on your training agenda. The training schedule provided here is merely to allow mastery of the technique whilst providing a wide variation to enrich the experience and to show you what is possible. For specific goals you may wish to tailor the approach, but the information provided will be sufficient for you to do so.

The manual is self contained and extra reading on the topics is not necessary for mastery. The reference section provides a list of resources that were relied upon for completion of the work; however, some sections are purely the fruit of the author's work and innovation, and thus have no references elsewhere. The interested reader may wish to explore the references but to emphasise the point, it should be noted that for practical use of the techniques extra reading is not necessary.

A Note regarding wording convention

The reader should note that the convention of "he/him" was used rather than "he/she him/her" in order to avoid confusion when presenting the techniques. The main goal of this manual is to provide a clear set of instructions and avoiding ambiguity is thus paramount. This is the only reason for choosing the "he/him" convention- there is no gender pre-requirement for this manual and so the reader can think in whichever term is appropriate to her or him irrespective of the written word.

Instructions

For optimal use of this manual and one's time, the reader is recommended to follow the instructions herewith without exception:

1. Have a purpose in mind: what do you aim to get out of this book and what do you hope to achieve with the techniques provided?
2. **Read the book in the order in which it was written.**
3. Become well versed with the techniques presented in each part before moving on to the next.
4. Ensure that the training schedule of each section is followed exactly as instructed.
5. Persevere with the training, especially the first part of the book which deals with concentration. There are certain barriers that need to be broken before everything falls into place. The techniques presented work but practise is necessary for mastery.
6. Incorporate the techniques in your everyday life- just experiment, you do not have to rely on them at first, just test them out.

Much like driving a car, at the beginning it appears to be a great deal of multiple actions, thoughts and techniques put together that appear insurmountable, but with little practise it becomes second nature. The techniques in this book are exactly the same; your aim should be to make them second nature. Just like drivers, there are mentalists out there that have mastered some of the techniques, if they can do it so can you- the only components required are a good technique, motivation and diligent practise.

Character is the ability to follow through on a resolution long after the emotion with which it was made has passed

Brian Tracy

Part 1-Concentration

If you chase two rabbits, both will escape.

Chinese Proverb

Aims

- Improve concentration by practising attention-focusing techniques and meditation.
- Use meditation to induce deeper states of mind which facilitate relaxation, learning, reasoning and recall.

Why concentrate?

The Oxford Dictionary definition for concentration is as follows:

'The action or power of focusing all one's attention' & *'dealing with one particular thing above all others'*

Concentration is the cornerstone of existence without which no thinking can take place, without thinking there can be no learning.

With the advent of communication, entertainment and gaming technologies, modern society appears to be cramming an ever greater amount of tasks into an already multi-tasked existence. An executive talking on the phone via speaker whilst reading through his latest e-mails on the blackberry all whilst pedalling on the exercise bike keeping an eye on the markets as displayed on the television above his head and the enjoying the background beats of the music played in the aerobics class joined to the repetitive sounds made by his fellow gym enthusiasts on their lunch break- this is not an absurd example of city life but rather an almost prototypical example.

Multitasking can be useful when trivial tasks are undertaken; these tasks should be characterised by having little to no need for reasoning (like cleaning or washing the dishes) but the habitual use of multitasking as a way of getting more things done often results in the opposite. Some tasks should not be bundled with others and the tendency to always attempt to save time by doing more things concurrently can hinder one's ability to concentrate.

The limits to multitasking are clear when one realises that learning is done by reading or listening to the information being relayed, this information then needs to be reasoned and subsequently it needs to be memorised. The ability to capture the information in the first place is directly proportional to how much attention you provided.

Without concentration, the above sequence breaks down. With partial concentration, the above sequence takes longer to complete and because it takes longer it may cause the student unnecessary frustration and perhaps even the misguided belief that the material is "too difficult". Such negative cycles can be vicious and self-sustaining; after some time it can affect one's ability to learn and thus limit potential and performance later in life.

Some mental tasks cannot be completed without complete attention to the task at hand; for example a speed reader that boasts a reading speed of 2000 words per minute cannot allow his attention to wander; if he does, for every second he lacks attention to the tasks he would miss 33 words, for every 3 seconds he would miss a key paragraph and thus a key concept, and the overall outcome would be a poor result on the comprehension of the material and thus necessitating the need to repeat the reading of the material.

Imagine trying to understand a complex scientific theory or a complex business deal while your train of thought keeps getting interrupted by other intruding ideas generated internally by you or externally by your environment. Every time you sense that you are about to have figured out a step in the structure an interruption enters and makes you lose the place and thus the entire portion of that journey has to be repeated to arrive at the same realisation in order to proceed to the next step in the structure. With constant interruptions it is simple to see that lack of attention requires the inefficient revisiting of ideas that have already been reasoned and greatly hinders any momentum in the thinking process which ends costly in terms of time. It is much like climbing up a treacherous mountain whilst talking on the phone which inevitably leads to stumbling and falling down the mountain only to latch on to a rock for safety before recuperating and heading upwards again but having to cover the same ground all over again.

Concentration is the first part of the manual because everything that follows relies on the user's ability to focus his attention on the task at hand- the deeper the ability the greater the benefit!

It is perhaps the most challenging task to achieve due to our way of life but it is a challenge that must be undertaken to reap the full benefits from all that follows.

Scientific Evidence

Attention is one of the most heavily researched topics in psychology and cognitive neuroscience; the history of research dates back to the 1850s but earlier cultures and religions have experimented with this topic for thousands of years, though by a deeper approach to the concept, namely- meditation. It is one topic that appears to feature equally in most major religions and proposed paths to spiritual enlightenment are claimed to be paved by the stones of meditation. We aim to use the techniques of old, which have been experimented with for millennia, whilst relying on the scientific rigor to rationalise our approach.

Meditation refers to the practise of training the mind to induce a deeper state of conscious awareness in order to achieve a goal, be it enlightenment, calm relaxation, deep thinking or other.

Meditation has been the focus of increased scientific research since the 1930s. Since then a copious amount of publications suggest links between various meditation methods and changes in metabolic rates, blood pressure, respiration, brain activation, attentional allocation, improved healing, reduced anxiety and improved emotional balance. These results have led the scientific community to introduce the use of several meditation techniques in clinical treatments of stress, disorders and pain reduction.

Recent scientific evidence even leads some authors to suggest that the ability to focus our attention today may have been an evolutionary response to the practise of meditation by earlier ancestors- a Baldwin effect (Baldwin effect is a theory in evolutionary biology suggesting a selection process in learnt abilities that make them innate for future generations) applied to attention and memory (see "Did Meditating Make Us Human?" by Matt J. Rossano).

Most importantly, recent scientific research suggests that meditation may increase attention spans. It is this evidence combined with the beneficial side effects that should motivate us to use meditation as a method to improve our concentration and so our ability to learn.

Levels of the mind

The brain is believed to function on different frequencies with each corresponding to a state of mind. These are classified as follows:

1. **Delta**- up to 4Hz, associated with deep sleep.
2. **Theta**- 4-8Hz, associated with drowsiness.
3. **Alpha**- 8-13Hz, associated with relaxed awareness.
4. **Beta**- 13-30Hz, associated with being alert and active.
5. **Gamma**- 30-100+Hz, associated with cross modal sensory processing.

It is the Alpha frequency that we should aim to attain for the purposes of learning.

Benefits of meditation or concentration training

- Lower blood pressure.
- Favourable changes in brain activity.
- Ability to focus more of our attention on a given task.
- Better executive function.
- Joys of relaxation and deep states of awareness.
- Enhanced creativity.
- Enhanced health and well being.
- Longer attention spans.

Techniques

This section introduces the techniques to allow the user to improve his concentration and reap the benefits of meditation. The techniques should be practised daily, preferably 3 times a day, consisting of two long sessions and one short.

The following instructions should be kept in mind when working on each technique:

1. The techniques should be performed sitting on a comfortable chair or lying down. The former is preferred since the latter can often cause the practitioner to fall asleep (which does not count as a completed training session).
2. Training time should be at least one hour after a meal (to allow for proper digestion) and at least two hours before going to bed (to avoid a state of high alertness before attempting to sleep).
3. Meditation is the art of letting go. Thoughts will always come, and meditation is the process of letting them go.
4. The practitioner should therefore avoid unnecessary anxiety that is caused by thinking: "this is not working, my mind is not clear, so many thoughts are distracting me...etc". The aim is to be in an environment that allows you to notice these thoughts and having the ability to let go of them.
5. The thoughts will surely come back, usually within seconds of you letting go but the practise is to let go of them again without having to react to them.
6. Remember this is time that you set aside for practise, so do not allow the ego to get in the way and suggest that you are wasting time. Letting go of the thoughts develops a skill that allows one to easily tune out that which you deem unimportant. This skill can take a while to develop but the benefits are worth the time spent.

7. Do not expect anything amazing to happen, this will involve your ego and desires and hinder your practise. Just follow the technique without thinking too much about it or what it means. Pondering and reflecting can be done before or after but never during.
8. Persevere, it will be difficult at first but easier as you progress and, once the main concept is understood, it will be almost automatic.

Technique 1- Mantras

Mantra chanting is a very popular technique in eastern traditions which was popularised in the west during the 1960s. The idea is to repeat a phrase, prayer or syllable over and over either vocally or in one's mind. This repetition has a very calming effect on the mind and is a simple tool to use since sounds are easy to repeat in your mind or vocally (as opposed to visualising or remembering a smell in your mind for example). The procedure is as follows:

1. Choose a mantra you will repeat; common choices are LAM, VAM, RAM, YAM, HUM, SHAM, OHM. [Choose one].
2. Set an alarm to ring after 20 minutes.
3. Sit comfortably with your feet flat on the floor and your hands resting on your thighs, eyes closed.
4. Take a deep breath, hold it for 10 seconds, and then breathe out. Repeat 3 times.
5. Now begin slowly saying the chosen mantra **in your mind**, not vocally. The pace should be calm and slow. Say you chose LAM; simply repeat it over and over: LAM.........LAM...........LAM.........
6. When thoughts intrude (and they will), just let go. When they come back, let go again and again without reacting, without

analysing the reason why the thoughts recur. Just let go and continue repeating the mantra, all slowly and calmly.

Variations

1. If the environment permits, you can experiment with a vocal repetition of the mantra, try to make the pronunciation of each mantra as long as your exhalation, and then breathe in and repeat.
2. You can move away from a syllable to a word or a prayer. The aim should be to stick with what works best for you, and in meditation simplicity is usually best.

It is recommended to make a choice and stick to it, so do not keep changing your mantra- settle on one that is comfortable for you and use it exclusively.

Technique 2- Letters

Visual techniques are favoured by many, given most people's tendency to rely on this modality (compare how much time you spend on TV or PC versus smelling flowers). However, the technique presented here relies on the ability to picture a letter with the inner eye, an ability that some find difficult at first. The procedure is as follows:

1. Take a white piece of paper and draw in thick black colour a letter of your choice; those with religious beliefs may choose a letter from their religion's alphabet (this method was commonly used by Jewish Kabbalists). It is not important which letter, just that you are familiar with it.
2. Look at this letter for a minute, just look at it without any analysis.
3. Set an alarm to ring after 10 minutes.

4. Now sit comfortably with your feet flat on the floor and your hands resting on your thighs.

5. Close your eyes and picture the black letter on the white background, it is not necessary to see it clearly or fully, it is just something to focus your attention upon whilst letting all else go. (Do not stress, strain or force yourself to see the image; relax and attempt to focus on any glimpse, blur or feel that it left in your mind).

6. When thoughts intrude (and they will), just let go. When they come back, let go again and again without reacting, without analysing the reason why the thoughts recur. Just let go and focus on the letter.

Variations:

1. When you become more confident in your practise, you can skip the part of drawing the letter (which is there to assist your progression of inner visualisation skills).

2. You can change the colours of the letter or the background, but do not change during the practise itself. So if you choose white letter on blue background for example, decide this before you begin your session and continue with this combination until the session is complete.

3. Increase the time gradually to 15mins, 20mins, 30mins.

Apart from improving your concentration, this technique trains your abilities to visualise pictures in your inner mind; this is going to be of great use when we introduce some of the memory techniques, increasing their effectiveness substantially.

Technique 3- Breathing

Breathing techniques play a key role in the meditative practices of
Indian Yoga and Chinese Qigong. There is a great deal of variety in
the teaching approaches and some conflicts depending on the branch
of the art practised. The subject is deep and the subtleties of each
technique can take a long time to master. The aim of this manual is
to be practical yet effective, hence the technique introduced below is
the one that has shown to be the easiest to master whilst being
valuable in terms of the results produced.

The technique is sometimes called "Buddhist breathing" or simply
"abdominal breathing" and the procedure is as follows:

1. Set an alarm to ring after 10 minutes.
2. Sit comfortably with your feet flat on the floor and your
    hands resting on your thighs, eyes closed.
3. Breathe in whilst allowing your abdominal area to expand,
    breathe out whilst pushing your abdominal area in.
4. The breaths should be slow and natural, you should not force
    your stomach in or out, the movement should be without
    tension.
5. Progress slowly and do not tense, begin with 5 seconds for
    the in breath and 5 seconds for the out breath and allow for
    longer if you are able to do so (7-10 seconds for in and out);
    the key point is not to tense and not to force it to happen.
    This movement is very natural (it is how one breathes as a
    baby until early childhood) and can be relearned with
    practise. Tension defeats the purpose and can have
    undesirable effects.
6. When thoughts intrude (and they will), just let go. When they
    come back, let go again and again without reacting, without
    analysing the reason why the thoughts recur. Just let go and
    focus on the abdominal area moving in and out with your
    breathing.

At the beginning, the physical method needs to be learnt. With 10 minutes every day, a reasonable comfort with the technique can be attained in 2-3 months, but each person is different and timelines should not be the gauge. It is whether you feel relaxed and focused that should signal whether you are progressing along the correct path.

Keys

1. DO NOT FORCE THE BREATH.
2. DO NOT TENSE: if you feel you are tensing, let go.
3. Allow the air to flow in and out naturally, expanding on the in breath and contracting on the out breath.

Variations

1. After practising for 6 months and when you are comfortable with the technique, you can proceed by focusing your attention 3 inches below your navel (usually measured by placing three fingers under the navel). According to Traditional Chinese Medicine, positioned there is a vital pressure point that is linked to the energy store of the body (Dan Tian). The breathing should continue as before, expanding on in, contracting on out.
2. After practising the above navel variation, and if the practitioner senses warmth within the inner abdominal region, he can proceed by focusing his attention in the middle of his abdominal area (directly behind the pressure point 3 inches below the navel). As before, simply focus the attention on that point inside the body and let go whenever distracting thoughts occur. The breathing should continue as before, expanding on in, contracting on out.

Technique 4- Countdown

We tend to use numbers frequently in our everyday life and the notion of countdown tends to solicit an expectation of an event to follow. This technique is simple to complete and involves a dynamic audio and visualisation processes which progress according to your thoughts. The procedure is as follows:

1. Set an alarm to ring after 10 minutes.
2. Sit comfortably with your feet flat on the floor and your hands resting on your thighs, eyes closed.
3. Begin with 100 and slowly countdown to 1 waiting approximately 3 seconds between each number. Try and picture the number (black number on white background) as well as saying it in your mind (not out loud).
4. Do not count the seconds between each number, just get into a comfortable rhythm and count down. 100...99...98...97 etc (counting in your mind and visualising at the same time). The slower you count down the better.
5. When thoughts intrude (and they will), just let go. When they come back, let go again and again without reacting, without analysing the reason why the thoughts recur. Just let go and focus on the countdown.
6. Once you reach 90, with every thought that distracts you, let go and return to 90. For example: 93...92...91...90...89...88...thought...90...89...88...87...86...thought...90... etc.
7. Do not let the fact that you are going over and over back to 90 because of repetitive thoughts, distract or disturb you. You should also avoid analysing the thoughts-- just let go.

With practise, this technique will allow you to measure your progress by realising how long you can countdown without any distracting thought.

Once you have mastered the technique and can proceed to 1 easily within the 10 minutes session, begin with 200 and increase as necessary.

Variations

1. Some variations of this technique include counting the breath. For each out-breath, you countdown one number. For example: breathe in/breathe out-100, breathe in/breathe out-99, breathe in/breathe out-98 etc... Every time you lose count or allow a thought in, go back to 90. This variation is favoured by some but can complicate the exercise too much and is not recommended to be used until mastery of the basic technique is achieved.
2. Some variations include using only the visual countdown or only the audio countdown but not together. Again, this should be practised only once the basic technique is mastered.

Technique 5- 3D objects

This is another visualisation technique that builds on the previous by introducing a 3-dimensional object compared to the 2-dimensional nature of visualising a letter or a number. This practise helps the development of the inner eye, which is extremely useful for memory techniques as well as mental arithmetic.

The easiest objects to begin with are items that are viewed on a daily basis, the choice you make should ensure there is a lively colour involved and distinct dimensions (rather than thin and flat). For this example we will pick an orange:

1. Set an alarm to ring after 10 minutes.

2. Sit comfortably with your feet flat on the floor and your hands resting on your thighs, eyes closed

3. Visualise the orange in your mind's eye. Try and make the image as clear as possible but do not strain nor try too hard. Picturing it on a neutral background tends to help, for example, picture a white space with nothing in it but a large orange.

4. When thoughts intrude (and they will), just let go. When they come back let go again and again without reacting, without analysing the reason why the thoughts recur. Just let go and focus on the Orange.

Variations

1. Try other items that you hold and see regularly, some examples are: lemon, apple, strawberry, geometrical shapes (pyramid, sphere). The desired object should have attractive colours (1 or 2 colours, but not more at this stage).

2. Once mastery of the above is achieved, try more complex shapes and visualise them with several colours, for example a Red and Blue Stellated Dodecahedron.

3. There are some schools of meditation that attempt to use deep states of consciousness to visualise higher dimensional objects (4D+). Since this is not possible with our current perception of reality, the exercise begins with a concept, focusing your attention on the "feeling" of a 4D object pushing away all other thoughts and ideas. This practise is extremely advanced and should not be attempted until the basic technique is mastered (even at that point it should only be experimented occasionally without a large investment of your time unless measurable results occur). At a deep level of meditation one is able to make sense of the concept of 4D and view a representation that makes the practitioner believe a visualisation has been achieved- though replicating the

image is not possible on paper nor at active states of mind after the session is complete.

It is important to note that the item should be visualised easily, if constant thought needs to be invested in trying to visualise it, then the practise is wasted. That is why it is advisable to begin with simple objects and then proceed to more complicated ones.

Technique 6- Smell

To the author's knowledge, this technique has not been covered by previous work on the subject of meditation; it uses an important sense that is often neglected but whose significance in mental performance is substantial. The idea is to use the memory of a strong pleasant smell and to meditate only on it. This allows you to gain the ability to use smells just as you use sounds or pictures in your inner mind, and it is a truly powerful tool in enforcing some of the memory techniques which will be introduced later in the book. The sense of smell is a powerful trigger, and, once the technique is mastered, whole scenes (including inputs from the other senses) unfold simply due to the trigger the smell provided. An example could be a scene of you on holiday walking on a quiet beach; recalling the precise smell of the ocean then enhances your recollection of the scene allowing it to become much more vivid. Mastery of this technique will make the concept of visualisation take a completely different meaning and experience.

The technique is as follows:

1. Set an alarm to ring after 10 minutes.
2. Sit comfortably with your feet flat on the floor and your hands resting on your thighs, eyes closed.
3. Choose a pleasant smell you would like to work with, make sure it is something you can recall easily or have experienced

recently, for example the smell of freshly baked bread or cooking pancakes.

4. Focus your attention on the smell. There is no need to visualise or remember the experience, just focus on the smell.

5. When thoughts intrude (and they will), just let go. When they come back let go again and again without reacting, without analysing the reason why the thoughts recur. Just let go and focus on the smell.

Technique 7- Touch

This is another technique, which to the best of this author's knowledge, has not been made available in the literature yet. The idea is to train another modality that tends to be ignored in mental activities.

The sense of touch can trigger a very relaxing response and meditating on it can train the user to solicit these responses without the physical stimulus being present. The procedure is as follows:

1. Set an alarm to ring after 10 minutes.

2. Sit comfortably with your feet flat on the floor and your hands resting on your thighs, eyes closed.

3. Attempt to recall a pleasant touch sensation you might have felt in the past; some examples could be:

4. The feeling of the hot sand, as you were walking down a deserted beach.

5. Or, the ocean water trickling between your toes.

6. Or, a material such as silk, that produced a feeling of comfort.

7. Once you have chosen one sensation that suits you and that you can recall, begin focusing your attention only on the sensation.

8. Do not visualise the setting and the other stimuli which were present, focus only on the touch sensation; in example (a) above it is the calming warmth on your feet- nothing else. Your mind knows the origin of the sensation (i.e that it is from the sand that is on the beach on which you are walking), hence it will not be confused with another warmth sensation. Therefore, allow your attention to settle solely on the touch sensation.

9. When thoughts intrude (and they will), just let go. When they come back let go again and again without reacting, without analysing the reason why the thoughts recur. Just let go and focus on the touch.

Variations

Variations of the above technique can include whole body touch sensation, for example:

1. Swimming in tepid water on a hot day.
2. Relaxing in the sun.
3. Being immersed in a mud bath.
4. Being covered by a fur coat, or lying on a thick carpet.

The concept is simple and can be extended to any touch sensations you have felt that were gratifying and memorable.

Other variations of the technique include focusing on more boring touch sensations such as:

1. Running your fingers on sand paper.
2. Feeling a tree trunk.
3. Feeling the cool of a wall.

Such mundane sensations as the 3 listed above, can offer a good training session since the feeling they invoke is less thrilling and so requires greater effort in concentration.

Technique 8- Relaxing scene

This technique builds on the previous exercises and allows you to experience a full scene with all the feelings that your senses were able to capture. The procedure is as follows:

1. Set an alarm to ring after 10 minutes.
2. Sit comfortably with your feet flat on the floor and your hands resting on your thighs, eyes closed.
3. Try and think of a pleasantly relaxing scene that you would like to experience; a prototypical example would be sitting on a deserted beach by the water, feeling the waves wash over your body and then recede back to the ocean and the warmth of the sun sprinkling over your body until the next wave washes to the shore with a great whooshing sound.
4. You start the exercise by focusing on each individual sensation (i.e smell, touch, sound, view and taste) just once and then let go. Spend a few seconds on each modality and then move to the next step.
5. Then feel as though you are in the scene, this is now the point of focus, do not try and focus or shift from each individual sensation, instead just focus on being in the scene and experiencing the overall scene. When you are able to just feel as though you are there, the individual sensations will creep in on their own- all you need to do is maintain the feeling of being there as your point of focus.
6. When thoughts intrude (and they will), just let go. When they come back let go again and again without reacting, without analysing the reason why the thoughts recur. Just let go and focus on the feeling of being there.
7. Essentially you are focusing your attention on one feeling here, it is just that this feeling is complex and carries several modalities within it.

To reiterate the key point of the technique above; after focusing on each individual sensation very briefly, you let go and focus only on the overall feeling of being there.

Technique 9- Background Sound

This technique aims to utilise noises that are present in one's environment and demonstrates to the practitioner how such sounds, that may cause frustration at times, can be equally soothing if a different interpretation takes place in the mind. Mastery of this technique would provide the practitioner with a substantially improved control of his environment, allowing it to affect him in the way that he chooses. This is a valuable tool for competitive performances or any pressure situations that take place in noisy environments. The procedure is as follows:

1. It is advisable to begin in a relatively quiet setting and progress to noisier setting as your skill improves.
2. Set an alarm to ring after 10 minutes.
3. Sit comfortably with your feet flat on the floor and your hands resting on your thighs, eyes closed.
4. Listen to any recurring noises in the room or environment in which you are situated. It can be the humming of the air-conditioner, the sound of trains on the tracks or cars on the road...etc.
5. Whenever that sound appears you will notice it and begin analysing its meaning. The aim of this exercise is to notice when you begin thinking about the sound and then, just let go of the thoughts. So for example, the sound of a car driving by is registered, and then your mind may begin to journey on the following type of thought loop:

"Why did I choose to live on a busy road, it's quite noisy, but it's good cause it's close to work, oh I forgot to file in the report, my boss won't like it, I better get in early and do it before he comes in, but early means a long queue for the bus, oh and this morning my seat was wet because it was raining heavily and someone must have left his umbrella there earlier, oh I should bring an umbrella tomorrow the forecast suggests it is going to rain....."

Perhaps not along this precise line of thought but the general pattern may seem familiar; the idea is to stop this train of thought before it begins and at least before it gathers steam. So the approach would be that whenever you hear the sound, you just let go, you hear the sound and nothing else follows, if thoughts come in just let go, do not analyse and do not search for meaning- just let go.

Variations

As your skill improves, you may choose to increase the challenge by trying noisier environments. However, it is important to ensure you have mastered the simple environment first.

Examples of more challenging environments would be:

- Busy train/bus/underground station.
- Airport.
- Market/Bazaar.

(But you must ensure that sitting there with your eyes closed does not compromise yours or others' security or safety).

The approach is exactly the same:

- Do not think of the sounds.

- Do not try and analyse them or figure out where they came from.
- Just allow the sounds to arrive and depart without any effect on your mental process.

Remember: meditation is the art of letting go, do not expect thoughts not to arise. The whole purpose of a session is to practise letting go and to enjoy the relief-sensation that this induces.

Training plan

"Strategy without tactics is the slowest route to victory.
Tactics without strategy is the noise before defeat".

Sun Tzu

The previous section describes the techniques that would help one improve his ability to concentrate; however, without a training plan the techniques are worthless. As with most skills, persistent practise is required before mastery is attained. The problem appears to be that most of those eager to gain the results often stop their practise after a major hurdle presents itself. This is perhaps the main reason why we are amazed when we see individuals performing mental feats; we believe that these feats are impossible because few get to achieve them and this occurs because few have the character to persist in the face of adversity.

It is therefore paramount to have a specific training plan in place and basic rules to enforce compliance with the training. Most importantly it is necessary to have a tool to measure progress in order to verify whether the approach taken is effective.

With concentration, measuring of progress is challenging since it is highly dependent on the environment, external factors, general mood of the day, worries/concerns recently experienced, as well as due to the difficulty in defining the unit of measurement. To achieve the task of measurement, we will use the countdown technique to plot how far down the countdown the practitioner was able to descend. This should not be done daily since such a period does not allow sufficient time for improvement; doing so fortnightly and plotting the results may be a reasonable time period. It should be noted that initial results are highly dependent on the personality of the practitioner; some people see quick initial improvement that plateaus rapidly whilst others may experience no progress until one day all the concepts seem to fall into place and a huge leap in progress is recorded. It is therefore advisable to train for at least 3 months before attaching any significance to the measurements.

Rules

1. **Train every day**- the refined skill of concentration is built gradually on previous days' progress. Missing a day can take you a several steps back and cause frustration due to apparent lack of progress. It is therefore paramount that the training is completed every day without fail; if urgent circumstances present themselves then the training can be reduced to just one 10 minute session.

2. **Do not try to catch up**- do not try to make up for a missed day by doing double the next day; this may overload your system and cause frustration and perhaps even make you feel as though this is a chore. It is certainly not a chore; these are relaxation exercises and should be viewed with anticipation just as much as one would anticipate a tasty meal or a good movie or finishing work on Friday. Regular practise is the key, do not overdo for the wrong reasons.

3. **Measure your progress every two weeks using the countdown technique-** As discussed above, progress can be measured using the countdown technique, i.e. by recording the lowest number the practitioner arrived at during the session once 10mins have elapsed. The training schedules below only include the countdown technique from week 5 onwards because it is advisable to have a month of training that does not involve any pressure of achievement. For some, this is a crucial component in gaining confidence with the ideas being taught.

4. **Follow the training schedules and continue your practise even after mastery-** below are simple training schedules that focus the first few months on the core techniques, those that

are simplest to perform and most effective. Once mastery has been achieved you can design your own schedule or continue with the one suggested. The important point here is that training should not be stopped after the 12th week; to maintain the skill gained would require regular practise, and, with concentration, the level of mastery is never finite- there is always a deeper experience that one can strive towards.

5. **Do not compare your progress with others-** concentration and relaxation are not competitive sports, once ego begins to interfere with the training, all efforts would have been wasted. Concentration is a means to an end; it is there to improve your ability to learn as well as to relax. Comparing progress is fraught with dangers since the person you are discussing with may have different views, may not be honest with his views or may discourage you altogether by suggesting something else to try.

Schedule

The schedule below requires the user to set aside 20 minutes in the morning, 10 minutes at lunch and 10 minutes in the evening. This may not be possible for all readers but it is encouraged for optimal results. If these three daily sessions cannot be completed on a regular basis then at the very least, practise once a day for 20 minutes. It should be noted that practising only once a day would result in a longer period before measurable progress takes place. This is not a bad situation if it is the only available choice, but the key is to be realistic with what is possible within one's schedule and execute regularly on that basis without fail.

Week 1-4

	Mon	Tue	Wed	Thu	Fri	Sat	Sun
Morning - 20m	Mantra	Mantra	Mantra	Mantra	Mantra	Mantra	Mantra
Lunch - 10m	Letter	Letter	Letter	Letter	Letter	Letter	Letter
Evening - 10m	Breathing	Breathing	Breathing	Breathing	Breathing	Breathing	Breathing

Week 5-8

	Mon	Tue	Wed	Thu	Fri	Sat	Sun
Morning - 20m	Mantra	Mantra	Mantra	Mantra	Mantra	Mantra	Mantra
Lunch - 10m	Count-down	Letter	Count-down	Letter	Count-down	3D objects	3D objects
Evening - 10m	Breathing	Breathing	Breathing	Breathing	Breathing	Breathing	Breathing

Week 8-12

	Mon	Tue	Wed	Thu	Fri	Sat	Sun
Morning - 20m	Mantra	Mantra	Mantra	Mantra	Mantra	Mantra	Mantra
Lunch - 10m	Touch	Letter	Count-down	Smell	Relaxing Scene	3D objects	3D objects
Evening - 10m	Breathing	Breathing	Breathing	Breathing	Breathing	Breathing	Breathing

Week 12-

	Mon	Tue	Wed	Thu	Fri	Sat	Sun
Morning - 20m	Mantra	Mantra	Mantra	Mantra	Mantra	Mantra	Mantra
Lunch - 10m	Touch	Letter	Count-down	Smell	Relaxing Scene	3D objects	Any technique
Evening - 10m	Breathing	Breathing	Breathing	Breathing	Breathing	Breathing	Breathing

Summary and Revision-Map

Key points

- Concentration is at the crux of capturing information.
- Meditation is the approach taken to improve concentration and relaxation.
- Apart from better learning and greater relaxation, there are also health benefits associated with meditation.
- Common to all approaches to meditation is the art of letting go.
- The techniques should be practised every day for 3 times a day according to the schedules.
- Persist with the schedule and measure progress every two weeks after week 4.
- Continue practise after completion of the 12 weeks, 3 times a day is optimal, once a day is the bare minimum.

Revision-Map

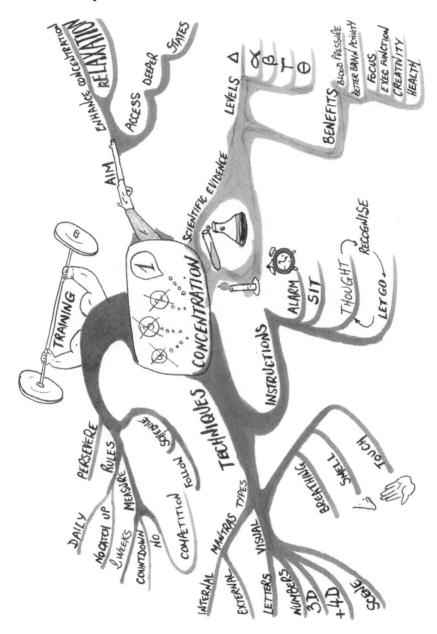

Part 2- Memory

Unless we remember we cannot understand.

Edward M. Forster

Aims

- Be able to immediately commit to memory any type of information.
- Be able to retain the information for the length of time that is dependent on its desired use.
- Make the process of memorisation fast yet effective and avoid the use of rote learning.
- Have incredible amounts of fun whilst memorising and so make learning a much more enjoyable experience.

Importance of memory

There are two advantages of having a bad memory; the first is that traumatic events fade quickly and have a weak effect over one's future whilst the second is, as Friedrich Nietzsche put it: *The advantage of a bad memory is that one enjoys several times the same good things for the first time.*

Upon further reflection it is clear that such advantages are also disadvantages when applied to the other extreme phenomena (the first to major positive events and the second to boring and unpleasant events).

It is quite simple, without memory of an event or experience, no learning can take place; and if no learning takes place no growth in one's abilities can materialise: you are left in a state of stagnation and inertia. That is an extreme, but it is easy to deduce that a weak memory will not allow one to reason deeper aspects of a topic since the basics remain a mystery.

Some of the techniques introduced in the concentration training will prove quite useful for memory; for example, the ability to visualise more clearly or to include smells, sounds and touch are extremely powerful mnemonics. Most importantly though, if the reader has reached this stage and has spent at least 4 weeks following the concentration training schedule, he would be in a better position to focus the mind on the task at hand and memory is largely driven by attention: when we provide our undivided attention, a signal in the brain indicate that an experience of nearly survival importance is being experienced and thus a record is made for future reference.

The concepts introduced in this part of the book will be an additional mechanism of ensuring that the memory of the event/experience is retained.

Photographic vs. Eidetic memory

There are some that wish they had a photographic memory, simply looking at something and being able to recall with clarity the information contained. Upon further reflection, the benefits of such an ability (whether this ability exists is subject to a great deal of controversy, and some believe that such a recollection only lasts seconds and fades shortly after) are questionable when one considers what memory is: the ability to recall is only one aspect, the deeper side is the imprint a memory makes on our thinking and character. It is not sufficient to have a picture of the information in your mind, it is the imprint of the reasoned understanding of a topic that allows you to then build on that foundation- this imprint is not a picture but a much deeper connection of neurons. It is akin to going into an exam with the textbook: the person that does this will have a poorer understanding of the topic and his ability to answer non-fact based questions on the topic would be limited since the information has not been reasoned and accumulated into the person's conscious awareness.

Recorded feats of memory

Below is a sample of recently recorded demonstrations of what a trained memory can achieve:

Category	Result	Record Holder	Year
Reciting Pi from memory	83, 431 decimal place	Akira Haraguchi	2005
Most binary digits memorised in one minute	240	Itay Avigdor	2006
Most binary digits memorised in 30 minutes	4140	Ben Pridmore	2007
Most cards memorised	59 packs (3068 cards) with only 1 error	David Farrow	2007
Time taken to memorise a single pack of cards	21.9 seconds	Simon Reinhard	2010
Most numbers memorised in one second	20	Ramón Campayo	2010
Most binary numbers memorised in one second	48	Ramón Campayo	2010

Scientific evidence

There are three general stages to memory:

1. Registering the information.
2. Storing the information.
3. Retrieving the information.

The types of memory are split into three major groups:

1. Sensory memory- a representative example of this type of memory is when glancing at a sheet of data and then glancing away; the first few milliseconds glancing away allows you to still see the data as if it was just in front of you, however this memory lasts for only a few hundred milliseconds and by the time you attempt to recall it the information is gone.
2. Short term memory- this is memory that can be recalled between a few seconds to a minute after first being encountered. Some research suggests that encoding of the information is mainly acoustic rather than visual.
3. Long term memory- through repetition (or the techniques presented in this chapter) information can be stored in long term memory- which refers to periods of years up to a lifetime. Research suggests that Long term memory is primarily encoded semantically.

The hippocampus is a part of the brain believed to be essential in the transferral of memories from short term to long term storage. Sleep is considered a crucial component in this process of consolidating information.

Early models for memory postulated that any short term memory that is kept in short term storage long enough (through repetition for example) would automatically get transferred to long term storage (this is the typical Atkinson-Shiffrin model). However, more recent studies suggest that excitement enhances memory by stimulation of hormones that affect the amygdala whilst excessive stress, which exposes the brain to cortisol, could hurt memory storage. It is therefore important to realise the effects that the state of mind has on your ability for long term storage and overall learning performance.

Without using any techniques, it is sensible to realise that lifestyle choices have a strong effect on cognitive functioning- crucial factors are regular and adequate amount of sleep, balanced diet, physical activity and limiting stress.

Assuming no stress factors, forgetting is still a natural process that the brain follows, the main factors are:

1. Cue-dependent forgetting- failure to remember the information due to the lack of stimuli that was present when it was first encoded.
2. Trace Decay- it is believed that new information causes a set of neurons to create a neurological memory trace in the brain- this trace naturally fades with time. However, with repetition the synapses experience a structural change after which the memory moves from being short term to long term. There are several competing theories for the existence of trace decay:
   a. Interference theory- competition/conflict between old and new information.
   b. Decay theory- disintegration of the neurochemical trace over time- it is believed that this happens in order to ensure that only the most important traces are kept so that brain works most efficiently for processes that are critical for survival or deemed significant.
   c. Organic- physiological damage or disease.

Following from the concepts above, "forgetting curves" are the name given to the exponential decay of the memory of newly learnt knowledge- these were discovered in 1885 by Hermann Ebbinghaus. The discovery suggested that forgetting naturally has a known relationship with respect to time and in order to maintain the information in long term storage a rehearsal of the material is necessary before hitting major decay levels on the curve. The techniques of "spaced repetition" revolve around this concept and make rote or repetition-type learning more optimal by only reviewing at pre-determined periods that are in-line with the forgetting curves- so that time is not wasted on unnecessary repetition, as well as not allowing the information to disappear from conscious recall.

Forgetting curves can be described mathematically using the following formula:

$$\text{Memory Retention} = e^{-\frac{t}{s}}$$

Where:

"t" is the amount of time elapsed since learning the material

"S" is the strength of the initial encoding

We can easily affect the two variables in this formula and this is the basis of the techniques introduced in this part of the book. We increase "S" by using memory techniques that encode the information as being of high importance or significance- this is done through exaggeration and nonsensical visualisation. We then affect "t" by reviewing the information at optimal times to ensure storage is transferred to long term memory.

General concepts

Improving one's memory using a system has several key ingredients that are consistent across all the different methods that are presented in the literature. In this section we introduce these key ingredient and the rules with which they must be applied. It is crucial to again point out that these rules were established after decades of research and experimentation, and have been shown to be the optimal combination of steps in terms of retention as well as speed and efficiency.

Key principles

In order to remember something we need to first pay attention to it (hence we covered concentration in the first chapter), but we tend to only pay attention to topics or events that are of interest to us or are of survival significance. The idea behind most memory system is to 'trick' the mind into believing that the concept being memorised is out of the ordinary (thus interesting) or so shockingly unusual that it triggers primal emotions (survival significance). It is simple to notice then that any memory system would need to take the information and add spice or emotion to it before it can be committed to memory. We therefore introduce the 'tools' that would allow us to implement a system:

Images- Images are the crux of the memory techniques presented here. Use objects that the words represent or convert abstract concepts into images- then apply the techniques.

Link method- this is the method used to take two pieces of information at a time and connect them together, replicating the natural way in which new information is incorporated by the brain.

For example say you wanted to memorise a list of items, one way to do so is to link each item to the next:

Shoes, sofa, hose, coffee, iPad, orange, kettle

In essence we would need to link shoes to sofa to hose to coffee to iPad to orange to kettle. The idea is to link each item we do not know to an item we already know. There are several ways to do this:

Logic- if a logical connection exists between the items and the list does not allow the possibility for confusion- logic can be used to remember it. Unfortunately, the list above does not have an obvious logical representation and the list is not short so a different tool needs to be employed:

Creative linking - this is the 'glue' of memory systems: using this technique, one can link any items in any order without the need for a logical connection between them. The idea behind this method is to employ the 2 basic principles behind the imprint of any memory:

    a. The need to pay attention- we do so by creating exaggerated pictures that are unusual, full of colour, have nonsensical action, are novel and interesting- most importantly they need to be absurd.
    b. The need to make the picture of primal significance (through emotions) - in connection with the above, the picture that we create needs to evoke emotions (e.g. hilarious, scary, disgusting, confusion, lust etc).

To use the list of items above as an example, we begin with the first item, shoes. Picture a pair of shoes in your mind, now link it with the next item, sofa. To do this you should create a picture that contains a sofa and shoes in the most absurd manner you are able to imagine. An example could be a giant pair of shoes sitting on a sofa with the

shoelaces folded behind the back of the top of the shoe (imitati
person with his arms crossed behind the head and hands resting on
the back of the neck). The key in this picture is to make it vivid and
exaggerated- so visualise in your mind as clearly as possible the
details of the shoe (colour, is it new?, is it clean/shiny or muddy
etc... – no need to ask these questions just make your picture vivid in
this manner) and exaggerate the proportion of the shoe compared to
the sofa- so the shoes are massive and resting on a tiny sofa that
seems to be about to balk under the immense weight of the shoes.

Let us move to the next item, hose; we now need to link sofa to hose,
so picture a hose in the garden that is watering the flowers with sofas
instead of water: millions of sofas are being released from the hose
and are landing on the flowers, being absorbed and helping them
grow. The key here is to picture lots of sofas (or even better, lots of
giant sofas) emerging from the hose- try and vividly picture the exit
point of the hose being stretched every time a bunch of giant sofas
exit from it- imagine how painful this experience must be for the
hose.

At this point the reader may question the sanity of the author; it is
important to realise that this approach to memorising may seem
absurd to those who have never encountered it before, but with
practise this is one of the greatest exercise in imagination one could
perform and it provides many mentalists with a pleasurable
experience whilst accumulating desired information at the same
time. Readers that have reservations against using this approach due
to the ridiculous thoughts it requires, are missing out on an
incredible experience- to have fun at the same time as learning. Note
that all mentalist and participants in memory championships use
systems that include some form of the above general approach.

Moving on to the next item, coffee; imagine a hose on his lunch
break sipping a Giant Starbucks coffee, try and smell the aroma that

this giant cup is diffusing, try and imagine how pleasurable this hot coffee must feel to the hose.

Proceeding with the next item, iPad; imagine yourself having your morning coffee with a stack of giant iPads on a plate, you then take an iPad, fold it in half with your fingers, dip it in the coffee and eat it. Try and imagine the taste it would have, the hard texture and the disgusting taste of metal, hot plastic and toxic chemical mixed with coffee- try and feel the disgust and the emotions this generates.

The next item is orange; imagine you received a present for your birthday, you unwrap it and you find a massive iOrange, you are tapping the front of the orange and the internet comes up, you start surfing whilst playing your favourite songs. Try and include how happy you were to receive this Orange as a present, how cool the touch screen functionality is etc...

The last item is kettle; imagine you are walking in an orange trees plantation and you are feeling hungry, but instead of oranges hanging from the tree there are lots of immense electric kettles. So, you climb on a tree and you pick up lots of kettles and put them in the front of your shirt. Imagine how scared you feel when you are hanging on an orange tree branch with a shirt full of immense kettles.

What comes after shoes?

After this demonstration, when the word shoes is mentioned, you should immediately have the funny picture of the shoes on the sofa appear in your mind. This picture then triggers the next picture of the sofas shooting out of the hose, which then brings the next picture of the hose drinking coffee, which leads to the next picture of the iPad dipped in coffee which then brings the iOrange and that then leads to you picking kettles from an orange tree.

The system is generally accepted as infallible; any such picture that could not be recollected is usually due to one or a combination of the following factors:

a. **The pictures were not vivid enough**- take your time when building the pictures, see them as clearly as possible. At the beginning this may take a while but after practise the pictures will be created as quickly as the information is being learnt- almost automatic.

b. **The details were not exaggerated enough**- make it absurd, the main qualifying criterion is that this is something that you would not see in real life or on your day to day experiences.

c. **Your state of mind was not conducive**- it is important to relax when learning (hence the first section of this manual focuses on concentration and meditation) - stressful times can release hormones that affect the chemical activity in the brain which can impede any connections made at the time.

Imagination is infinite- The greatest aspect of this method is that the possibilities are truly infinite and are limited only by the current capabilities of your imagination. The reader should not be startled if he is under the belief that he lacks imagination- this is a trait that is available to all, only some have personalities that allow them to portray it more than others. With practise this can be activated and improved. It is important to note that imagination should not be seen competitively- it is a very personal trait which should be shared only as much as you are comfortable and only for the aim of showing others the dimensions to which this trait can be expanded to.

It is sometimes interesting to talk or e-chat with others regarding the links created for a list of similar items to see if there are ideas you can incorporate into your toolbox. This is not necessary since with practise this skill will become freer and will flow to directions (via connections with other ideas in your mind at the time) you never knew existed.

A simple source of absurd ideas and nonsensical action can be found in cartoons, some prototypical examples are:

a. Animaniacs
b. The Ren & Stimpy Show
c. Bugs Bunny
d. Road runner
e. Sylvester and Tweety Bird
f. Goofy
g. Daffy Duck

If you have young children (older than 2 years, since TV exposure before that age is suggested to have adverse effects on the child's development) this is an excellent opportunity for bonding whilst at the same time releasing your mind from the recently learnt limits to which it has become accustomed to.

Objects are best- when converting words into pictures it is best to use objects as these can be visualised quickly and effortlessly (concentration exercises from the previous section help to make this process even more efficient. However, in some cases the words will involve abstract ideas rather than a physical object; in such a case, depending on which is better, one can either (examples provided in the sections below):

a. Convert into a similar sounding word that is itself an object.
b. Convert into an object that the word reminds of, or is related to.

The first picture that comes to mind is usually the best- for the sake of efficiency and to avoid time wasting on trivial decision making, it is recommended to pick the first reasonable picture that comes to mind rather than trying to find the best possible choice.

Rules

1. Exaggerate your images in:
    a. Proportion
    b. Size
    c. Quantity
    d. Absurdity of the action
    e. Or all of the above at the same time if possible.
2. Colours- make picture colourful.
3. Make the pictures shocking and absurd- it can definitely not be something you would see on a day to day- the brain has to believe this is something incredible that needs to be retained for future reference.
4. Sounds- incorporate sounds into the image in order to enforce the picture or the action taking place.
5. Smells- as mentioned before, smells are very powerful memory triggers, incorporate smells in your links where possible.
6. Emotions- incorporate emotions into the picture; they have to match the action or scenario taking place. In general the best are fear, lust and humour.
7. See the images vividly.

Gluing toolbox for linking

1. Substitution- replacing one object with another, for example we replace the orange with the iPad in the example listed above.
2. Large/Small- Making one object larger than it really is- for example the shoes were gigantic in the first picture.

3. Lots/Few- Involving a large number of the relevant object, for example the sofas shooting out of the hose were in their millions. The reader should note that saying millions whilst you create your picture would make you believe that this is how many there are and would immediately register as unusual- there is no need to count or focus too much on whether it looks enough- believing there are millions is sufficient in making the brain register this event as important and unusual.

4. Action- The actions should be exaggerated and nonsensical-eating the iPad after dipping it into the coffee is the example used for the list above. This should be an action you would not do in real life- something extreme and out of the ordinary.

5. Emotion- Involving emotion is extremely powerful, for example the fear of falling off the orange tree because you were carrying a shirt full of kettles as presented for the list above.

6. Change proportions- for example the immense coffee that the simple hose was drinking from was used for the list above, this mismatch in proportion is also a powerful tool to signal the importance of the picture and the need for the brain to register it.

7. Involve yourself in the picture- the example above involved you eating iPads dipped in coffee for breakfast- this image incorporates emotions (disgust) which becomes even more memorable due to the fact that we tend to remember better events that involve or affect us. It is our brain after all and the brain has a selfish survival mechanism- all that affects its existence should be recorded.

Visualising words

Words are easy to visualise since they provide a concept that, at times, is represented by an object or can at least be logically associated with an object. The approach to memorise words is as follows:

1. If the word represents an object simply visualise the object- for example the word apple would be visualised as such.
2. If the word cannot be represented by an object, for example "Friday" then:
   a. Convert to an object that is represented by a similarly sounding word, for "Friday" this might be "Fried hay". Or,
   b. Convert to an object that the word reminds you of, for example "Friday" might remind you of the movie "Friday the thirteenth" so you may choose to use Jason's mask or Jason himself if you can visualise it vividly enough. Or,
   c. If "Friday" has a personal significance to you which is immediately associated with an object you may choose to use that. The key point is that there are no limits, anything that reminds you of the word and if it can be visualised well it is a reasonable choice.
3. The larger your vocabulary, the more choices you have and the quicker the picture can be completed. The reader should note that with practise, vocabulary can be easily increased and so memory would improve, not only due to sheer practise of the method and imagination, but also due to the knowledge that has already been accumulated which then better facilitates the build up of further memories.
4. A note for multi-lingual readers: for those conversant or with knowledge of words from more than one language, this process is even quicker since the vocabulary that one can use for this method need not be restricted to one language. It can

even be mixed, so one word can be an object from one language whilst another word is an object from yet another language. It does not matter, the act of attention and exaggeration registers the relevant information necessary to interpret the picture in the way that was intended.

Visualising numbers and symbols

Numbers

Words were simple since they already represent a concept which in turn is either associated with an object or could easily be extrapolated in association to another object. Numbers and symbols however require a different approach which introduces the idea of a memory system:

1. For each number and symbol create a unique identifier which can be easily visualised (again, preferably an object).
2. Keep this identifier consistent, do not change it or replace it.
3. Avoid using similar identifiers that are related in concept (for example cup and mug).

The way to create a unique identifier is to convert numbers and symbols into words that represent unique objects that, going forward, will be used in our pictures to represent the number. We begin this exposition by introducing the phonetic alphabet:

Number	Phonetic Sound	Number	Phonetic Sound
1	T,D	6	SH, CH, J
2	N	7	K,G
3	M	8	F,V
4	R	9	P,B
5	L	0	S,Z

The idea of this approach is to associate with each number a consonant sound that exists in spoken words. We can then look at a list of numbers and easily convert them into words which in turn can be easily visualised. For example, say we are presented with the number 131485, its representation can easily be converted into letters using the table above, and the resulting list of letters could be one of the following permutations: "tmtrfl", "tmtrvl", "dmtrfl", "dmtrvl". These lists of letters can easily be bundled into words by adding vowels, for example "Time Travel" or "Dome Truffle" which can be visualised as a time machine (think of the DeLorean from the Back to the future trilogy) for the first permutation, the London millennium dome built out of truffles for the second.

It is simple to notice how, using this technique, any number can be converted to letters and these in turn to images. The key rules are as follows:

1. **Memorise the table above and do not change it**- unique identifiers must remain consistent for the system to work. An easy way to memorise this table is by applying some logic and some linking:

   1- Represents sounds that are due to letters of one down stroke (t and d).
   2- Is two down strokes (n).
   3- Is three down strokes (m).
   4- Four is R since the last letter is R.
   5- Offers no logic so link L (e.g. "Hell") with 5 (e.g. five fingers).
   6- Pronouncing Six with a full mouth can sound like Shix or Chix.
   7- Seven offers no logic so link k,g (e.g. sounds like "cage") with 7 (e.g. "Heaven").
   8- No logic so link f,v (e.g. "thief") and 8 (e.g.- "Hate").
   9- Nine can be inverted into a "b" and reflected into a "p".
   0- Zero sounds like Z-ro or See-ro, which reminds of "S" and "Z".
   Repeat this several times and test yourself to ensure complete control.

2. **Vowels and silent letters are ignored**- so 14 can be "Tyre" or "Tower" or "Tear" etc, it makes no difference. When the images need to be converted back into the numbers, list of words that make the image can only be interpreted in one way once the vowels are ignored. So if we memorised Tyre or Tower or Tear with something else it would always mean 14 and no other number- thus there is no ambiguity.

Note that it is the sound that matters not the letter itself-so the "c" in "Lace" would be representing zero since it sounds like "Lasse" whilst "c" in "Cat" would be representing seven since it sounds like "Kat".

3. **Expand your list**- it is advisable to extend the list above so that there is no need to break down the numbers into letters and then search for words that fit these letters. If the practitioner has a list of words for all numbers up to 100 then any two digits can easily be converted to a word and thus a step of thinking is eliminated and general speed is improved. We provide below an extended list up to 100, these should be memorised as above with either logic, association or rote-this is the only time we would excuse using rote since we are in the process of building a system that would eliminate any further use of this less efficient method.

A good approach would be to break the list into 10 groups of 10, memorising 10 each day- it is important to test every day the ability to recall what has been learnt until that point. Perfect recall of all 100 words makes everything else much more efficient and is highly recommended. The reader can use this list for ideas and can implement words that better suit him, the list below includes some common examples but it is always better to make this more personal and so alterations (subject to the general rules highlighted above) are highly recommended:

No.	Image	No.	Image	No.	Image
0	Saw	34	Mare	68	Chef
1	Tie	35	Mule	69	Shop
2	Knee	36	Match	70	Case
3	MO (from Simpsons)	37	MG car	71	Cat
4	Row (Rowing oar)	38	Movie	72	Coin
5	Lee (think Bruce Lee)	39	Mob	73	Gum
6	Shoe	40	Rice	74	Car
7	Key	41	Rot	75	Coal
8	Foe	42	Rain	76	Gauge
9	Pie	43	Rim	77	Coco
10	Taz	44	Roar (think lion)	78	Coffee
11	Toad	45	Rail	79	Cape
12	Tin	46	Raj (think India)	80	Vase
13	Dime	47	Rock	81	Fat
14	Tower	48	Reef	82	Fan
15	Till	49	Rib	83	Foam
16	Dish	50	Lace	84	Fur
17	Duck	51	Latte	85	Fly
18	Dove	52	Looney (think cartoon)	86	Fish
19	TP	53	Lamb	87	Fog
20	Nose	54	Lorry	88	Fava bean
21	Net	55	Lily	89	Fob
22	Nun	56	Leach	90	Bus
23	Gnome	57	Log	91	Boat
24	Honour (think Godfather)	58	Leaf	92	Bone
25	Nail	59	Lab	93	Palm (L is silent)
26	Hinge	60	Cheese	94	Bear
27	Nike	61	Sh*t	95	Bull
28	Knife	62	Chain	96	Beach
29	Knob	63	Jam	97	Pig
30	Maze	64	Shower	98	Bath
31	Mad	65	Jail	99	Pipe
32	Moon	66	Shisha	100	Thesis
33	A Mummy	67	Jockey	101	.....etc

Note that world memory competitors tend to extend this process to the thousands, in order to have a readymade representation of larger chunks of numbers. This approach speeds up the process of converting numbers into pictures and thus requires fewer pictures to memorise a given number. It is the difference of memorising 314159 as:

-MO, TIE, ROW, TIE, LEE, Pie – in single digits,

Versus

-MAD, ROT, LAB – using the list above,

Versus

-METEOR, TULIP – using a list extended to 100.

This is an important point for competitive mentalists since the ability to cut the total number of pictures into half or a third greatly improves speed, increases space for storage, better accuracy and less effort.

Note that extending the list is not a necessary part of the system but simply a method of applying it more competitively. For most purposes (except for competitions), 100 is an optimal list size to work with since it can be learnt quickly enough so as to not be too onerous a step in the learning of this system whilst still serving the purpose of encoding numerical data into images.

A final point to mention here, is that the lists (be it 100 or 1000) can easily be expanded by adding dimensions such as colours, locations, smells and sounds. We expand on this approach in later in this chapter.

Symbols

As with words and numbers, symbols can be converted into images as per the following rules:

1. If the symbol is a representation of an object then visualise the object.
2. Otherwise convert the symbol into an object by attempting to associate it to:
   a. Something the symbol represents- for instance the sign "$" can be associated with "wealth"- which can be represented by sacks of money for example.
   b. Something the symbol resembles- for example "*" looks like a snowflake- so a snowflake can be used in our visualisation.
   c. Something that the word for the symbol sounds like- for example "+" sounds like "pus" which can easily be visualised and evokes feelings of disgust.
3. The representation needs to be unique and consistent- once all the symbols that are needed to be learnt for a particular topic are known, the reader is advised to draw a table with the object that would represent it. It is important to remain consistent as it saves time and reduces the likelihood for error. For example, in the math section we would use the following:

Symbol	Image	Why
+	Pus	Plus sounds like Pus
-	Dennis the Menace	Minus sounds like Menace
=	Eagle	Equal sounds like Eagle
Division	Machete	Division is associated with cutting...
Power	Bodybuilder	Power associated with muscles
Integration	Interrogation light	Integration sounds like interrogation
Differentiation	Sock	Differentiating between the pairs of socks

The key is to draw up a list, write it down so a reference is available and then consistently apply it.

Adding dimensions

If the practitioner only mastered numbers 0-100, it is possible to multiply the entire list by factors of 10 without having to memorise or fix the list of words that corresponds to each number. The approach takes the current image that the number represents and adds the following dimensions:

1. Location
2. Colour
3. Action
4. Sound
5. Smell
6. Texture
7. Emotion
8. Shape

Below is a demonstration on how to apply the first 3 dimensions to expand the list, broadening further to the other dimensions is straightforward but is excluded for the following reasons:

a. Extending the list by adding dimensions makes the image much more complex and thus more difficult to memorise.
b. The more dimensions used, the more time it takes to build each image.
c. The added effort, difficulty and time can hinder overall performance.
d. Going past the first 3 dimensions requires accessing modalities that are not pictorial and are more difficult to keep fixed in mind for the purposes of memorising using systems. It is a possibility but requires persistent training in

combination with the concentration exercises, introduced earlier, that train these modalities.

Adding 3 dimensions

The first 3 extra dimensions will be added using the following formula:

VWXYZ

a. VW- Are the numbers we already know from 00-99.
b. X- This dimension is represented by location.
c. Y- This dimension is represented by colour.
d. Z- This dimension is represented by action.

Number	X	Y	Z
0	Jungle	Grey	Parachuting
1	Desert	Red	Showering
2	Lake	Black	Freezing
3	Field	White	Burning
4	Pigsty	Blue	Vomiting
5	Outer Space	Orange	Bleeding
6	Ocean	Green	Sweating
7	Mountain	Pink	Frying
8	Cloud	Brown	Sneezing
9	Football pitch	Yellow	Exploding

Examples

Say we wanted to memorise the number 33,980; we could split it into 3 parts: "3", "39" and "80" and memorise by linking them together since we already know the numbers from 0-100. The technique presented above allow us to capture this number with just one image instead of three, it is equivalent (in result but not in effort) to having a fixed list for all numbers from 0-99999. The procedure to building this image is as follows:

1. Begin with 33, the picture that represents this number is that of a mummy.
2. The next number is 9; the dimension corresponds to a location so this 9 determines that the image is taken on a football pitch.
3. The next number is 8; the dimension corresponds to colour, which is brown for number 8, so the mummy's colour is dark brown and is on a football field.
4. The last number is 0; the dimension corresponds to action, in the case of 0 this is parachuting, so the dark brown mummy is parachuting onto a football field.

To complete the example, assume that this number represents an internal extension at the office, this could easily be memorised by linking the person to the number. For example, say the person's surname was Jones- then all that is required is to link Jones to the picture we created for the number. An example link could be to think of a football field that is covered with lots of Indiana Joneses (instead of the usual green grass), and these Joneses are screaming out of fear as this gigantic dark brown mummy is landing on top of them crushing them.

Try the following number: 28,762, what picture would this number generate? [Pause to try and then read on]

A green Knife freezing its blade off on the top of a mountain; Say this was the extension for your boss, you may wish to picture your boss climbing a mountain and just as he lifts his head to view the peak he locks eyes with a menacing gigantic green knife that is shaking the frost off its blade- at that time you hear a loud scream of utter fear emanating from deep inside your boss' lungs.

Please note that the example above is not meant to be cruel nor to encourage challenging authority; it is simply there to demonstrate that the possibilities of your imagination are infinite and you **should not be bounded** by the same rules that govern your everyday behaviour- instead set your imagination free and let fantasy take over- the more extreme the better the link and thus the stronger the memory.

Other approaches

Extending dimension by 2: VWXY- VW as before whilst X is colour and Y is action

Extending dimension by 4: VWXYZA- VW as before whilst X is colour, Y is action, Z is smell and A is texture.

The permutation one chooses depends on which modalities provide the best results- this differs across people and so remains a personal choice. The key is to settle on an approach and apply it consistently thereafter- this is the key: without consistency, confusion will quickly set in and spoil the efforts made.

Needless to say that, in order to apply this method, the table representing the modalities that each number represents needs to be memorised and familiar.

Using this approach can take a while to master but is extremely useful as we will demonstrate in later sections with further application.

The reader should note that for a practitioner that has memorised words for each of the first 0-9,999 numbers, this method allows the possibility of stretching one image to contain a number with 7 digits (if extending to 3 dimensions) - in some countries this would correspond to a phone number: it is extremely impressive to convert a large chunk of numerical data (such as a phone number) to a single image. If the practitioner wanted to beat the current record for Pi he would only have to create 11,919 images whilst with a base of 10,000 numbers he would need 20,858. Even better, extending the list with 8 dimensions would mean only 6,953 images are needed.

The importance of repetition/review

This topic is frequently overlooked in the presentation of novel memory systems. It is true that by creating powerful links, a strong bond is created and the likelihood of forgetting it is reduced substantially, even after a long period of time has elapsed. The author recalls the first time he applied the system to remember a face (from a picture that was in a memory book)- the face and the name are still clear in his mind even though he only looked at the picture once, as well as the fact that nearly 20 years have elapsed. The reason was mainly due to the image created being ludicrous and the great deal of attention which was dedicated to the exercise. However, this is an exception rather than the rule; the way that memory is stored usually results in the elimination (at least from conscious awareness) of anything that was not extremely significant.

By repeating an action or revisiting a topic, the memory can become entrenched in medium to long term storage. The repetition has chemical and structural effects on the brain making the connections between neurons more efficient, thus requiring less energy to be used for the recall at future points in time. It also has the effect of signalling an important factor/task/fact that has become significant in a person's life (since it is experienced everyday) and the brain registers this by transferring the memory into longer term storage.

Most images created using linking, as presented above, disappear after 24-48 hours. Although different individuals react differently, this period appears to be the common norm. In order to incorporate the data into long term storage, a repetition (or revision) will have to take place before that window closes. The key point is to do the least amount of repetitions (for the sake of optimal use of time) but to ensure these are done before the memory fades away and has to be relearned.

Research on this topic indicates that the memory decay appears to follow a defined set of windows; by knowledge of these, one is able to optimally time the revision periods. For long term storage of memory it is therefore recommended to follow the procedure below:

1. Memorise the data with the techniques above (this is time = T_0).
2. Repeat the scene or image in your mind straight after, to ensure the data has been absorbed.
3. An hour later (T_0 + 1hour), attempt to recall the data and review the scene/image.
4. Ideally a couple of hours before going to bed, that is, T_0 + 12hours, (assuming the data was learnt in the day- otherwise simply perform 12 hours later) review again.
5. Review again the next day (i.e. T_0 + 24 hours).
6. Review once more a week later (i.e. T_0 + 1 Week).
7. Review once more 2 weeks later (i.e. T_0 + 2 Weeks).
8. Review once more 1 month later (i.e. T_0 + 1 month).
9. Review once more 3 months later (i.e. T_0 + 3 months).
10. Review once more 6 months later (i.e. T_0 + 6 months).
11. Review once more 12 months later (i.e. T_0 + 12 months).

The reader may look at the monolithic list above and be disheartened or overwhelmed; at this point, it is crucial to re-iterate that for long term storage extra stimulation is absolutely necessary. However, the task is much simpler than it appears in the list above, since all that is required is a brief glimpse at an image that is funny, absurd, enjoyable, fantastical and of your own creation- it takes mere seconds and can be seen as entertainment.

According to this author's experience, memory systems that promise long term memory results without repetition of the image/scene are not realistic and sometimes even omit certain points for marketing purposes (it is much less impressive to put on the cover of a self-improvement book, that several repetitions would be required for long term memory).

The difference between this and the rote memorisation method (the standard approach of re-reading and repeating until the information is committed to memory) is that the repetition in the rote method is required just to be able to absorb the information in the first place, whereas with the system above, the information is absorbed effortlessly on the first read-through. Furthermore, information learnt using the rote method would still require repetition as per the list presented above, since information learnt even by a large number of repetitions on day 1 is susceptible to elimination from longer term storage if not deemed important. It is therefore clear that the system provided herewith is far superior for absorbing information and repetition is only required for very long term storage.

The reader is strongly recommended to evaluate the importance of the information before dismissing the reviewing stage. It would be lamentable to initially spend time and effort studying and memorising, only to find that after a few months the memories dissipated and only a mild recollection of "previously knowing that you knew" has remained. A small effort would allow you to maintain the memories for a very long time, and this in turn would increase the general knowledge available for you to leverage on when making decisions, thinking as well as generating new ideas or solutions to problems.

Sleep is another important component for long term memory storage and so it is recommended to regularly get at least 8 hours of un-interrupted sleep every night, preferably going to sleep at the same time every night and doing so before 11pm. It is believed that memory consolidation happens mainly during sleep and interruptions can cause memories not to be transferred to long term storage.

Finally, the reader should note that if the purpose of the memorisation was short term (for example when performing mental arithmetic) a repetition or review is not necessary.

Being systematic and enforcing order

For the techniques to function optimally, order must be instilled; the aim should be to ensure there are no ambiguities. As an example, assume that the number 37 was converted to "Mug" and number 79 converted to "Cup"- these choices present an ambiguity because when the practitioner recalls an image that involves any form of drink-ware the possibility of getting the result confused increases- "Was it a pink tiger drinking from a cup or from a mug???"

It may not be possible to remove all ambiguities, especially when several types of information are being studied across numerous topics. Nevertheless, the aim should be to systematically design the memorisation approach to minimise the possibilities of ambiguity. This will be clearly demonstrated when the applications of the system are discussed in detail; for now, the reader is advised to ensure the following requirements are fulfilled:

1. Before memorising a major topic, break down the information into sub-components and convert it into items that can easily be pictured/imagined.
2. When breaking down the information, ensure that there is a unique identifier for each information bit- for example each letter, symbol, number, sound etc should have a unique image that is associated with it.

3. It is advisable to use a notebook to write down these unique identifiers; the table of mathematical symbols presented earlier in the chapter is an archetypical example.

The application section below will provide clear examples of this point and will clarify what is required.

Systems

This section focuses on the major systems that facilitate the fast and effective filing of information. The author introduces the different possible filing approaches which tend to serve different purposes and are optimal under different circumstances. The circumstances and their matching system are then introduced in the applications section.

Except for the link system, all other systems involve filing information by linking a new piece of information to something that is already known- this is called *pegging,* with the item that is already known aptly named as the *peg.*

The gluing concepts stay the same; the only difference is in the method with which these are filed in the brain.

Generally, there are 2 possible approaches:

1. Link all the unknown data together and link it to the topic's name
2. Link each data bit to something that is already known, this can be:
   a. A list of items and their order, that is already present in conscious memory.
   b. A room whose contents and their order of appearance are clear in conscious memory.
   c. A palace/city/country whose monuments or key attractions and their order of appearance are clear in conscious memory.
   d. A fictional room/palace/city/country whose fictional monuments or key attractions and their order of appearance are clear in conscious memory.
   e. A grid of items with their location in the grid already available in conscious memory.

Link system

This is a very free approach that is not limited by the size of the items/places you have available in your system. The approach allows linking a theoretically infinite list of items in a desired order with the ability to recall backwards or forwards but without allowing numerical positioning to be specified. So for example we could memorise a list of 1000 items and know that fridge comes after TV but we would not know that fridge is number 923 and TV is number 922. The application of this system is thus only merited when recollection of precise numerical position is not necessary.

The procedure for this method was already introduced above, but for completeness we summarise the steps:

1. What is the list for? e.g. a shopping list – this is crucial for correct filing and retrieval- without this, the reminder of what the 1st item is would be lost and hence the entire list could be jeopardised.
2. Link the first item to what type of list it is- for example link "shoes" to "shopping list".
3. Continue linking each item to the next until you reach the last item on the list.
4. Repeat the list in your mind a couple of times to ensure the links were good.

Step one is crucial and also points to the disadvantage of this system- if one item is forgotten the entire list could be lost. Generally this does not happen since knowing any item on the list would trigger memories of all the rest- for example in a list of 1000 items, if one has forgotten the first item but remembers that one of the items is "fridge", the links to the next and previous items (on the left and right of fridge) immediately come to mind and one can then work forwards and backwards from fridge to retrieve the list.

A better illustration of this point: if you hear "iPad", what are the two pictures that come to mind? It should be "orange" (to the right) and "coffee" (to the left).

Peg system

Creating a list of objects whose order (in numerical terms) you are familiar with allows you to then "peg" or file information in a way that would allow you to retrieve both the fact and the order (precise numerical position) with which it was meant to be memorised. It is called the peg system since we are essentially pegging a previously unknown item onto another item which is fixed and known. The clear advantages of this approach over the link system are:

a. The order of items as well as their exact numerical position can be recalled.
b. Forgetting one item does not jeopardise the entire list.

The mechanism involved here is present in all the other systems- namely the act of linking something new to something that is known. The trick involves creating plenty of lists with items that can be easily imagined/visualised and their numerical order of appearance captured. The rules for the creation of such lists are as follows:

1. Each item on the list must be easily pictured and is preferably an object.
2. The numerical position of the object is known.
3. There is no conflict with the other lists that were created and in current use.
4. There is a logical connection between the items on the list (i.e. they all belong to some group/type or they are all derived using a certain technique- e.g. the numbers 1-100 derived using the phonetic alphabet are a typical peg list).

Pegging involves the same glue that is used for linking, the procedure is exactly the same- make images that are wild, absurd, exaggerated, emotional, colourful etc... The only differences between using a peg list and a link system are that the peg list is known in advance whilst the link list is new, and that the former is established and has numerical values for each item whilst the latter does not.

Below are some examples of lists that can be easily created and allow efficient filing of information according to a certain order. The reason for having more than one list is to ensure better filing of information and to avoid using the same base for pegging everything. Perhaps the analogy of using a small stand to peg and dry all the clothes in the household make it glaringly obvious that having several stands will make the task of drying faster and more efficient. In the same way, pegging many new items onto one list all at the same time might cause confusion between which items belong to which list. For example, say one wanted to memorise a shopping list, the days' schedule, the list of presidents and some cricket scores- it is inevitable that some of the images would blur since each item on the peg list has 4 separate items pegged to it- corresponding to one item from each of the four lists.

The examples below should provide some inspiration on how to approach the creation of a new peg list; but for most day-to-day use, the below examples more than suffice in capturing and filing information without conflict. It is recommended again to be consistent, for example, the Number list should always be used for the shopping list and the Effigy list should always be used for today's calendar etc. (i.e. once it has been decided which list is used for which purpose, stick to it without further changes).

Numbers list

We have already presented the list of numbers up to 100 with their corresponding objects. This list can be used to remember another list by pegging each item on the new list to the already existing object in the number list. For example, say you have the following shopping list:

1. Eggs
2. Beans
3. Minced Beef
4. Milk
5. Soap
6. Lettuce

As demonstrated in earlier sections, this list can be memorised by linking each item to the next. However, the peg system involves pegging each of the items in the shopping list to an item on the number list:

Begin with the number 1, the corresponding item on the numbers list is Tie, so peg Eggs with Tie- perhaps try picturing cracking a tie on the fry pan's rim and a smaller tie falls out and starts to sizzle in the hot oil (make sure the tie you crack is enormous and disproportional).

Moving on to number 2, the number list contains the word Knee, so peg Beans to Knee- maybe try to visualise and feel how it would be like to walk around with a Knee that is made out of Bean- picture the Bean as large yet soft, connecting the thigh to the sheen- exaggerate the image and feel the discomfort this would bring.

Proceeding with the rest:

MO should be pegged to Minced Beef, Row should be pegged to Milk, Lee with soap and Shoe with lettuce.

Once the above images have been created and the number 2 is called out, it should immediately bring the image of a Knee which in turn triggers the nonsensical image of a person that has a Massive overgrown bean instead of a Knee.

It is clear that the user can then recall the items in order by going through from 1-100 or by looking up an item in a particular numerical position that is desired.

Effigy list

The list below was created by trying to picture the nearest object that looks like the number. Upon further inspection the reader may decide on better choices of images for some items- this is fine as long as it is applied consistently going forward.

Number	Peg
0	Smoke ring
1	Tree
2	Swan
3	Ant
4	Sail
5	Hook
6	Elephant Trunk
7	Boomerang
8	Grand Prix Track
9	Seahorse
10	Basketball net

As with all lists, it can be extended to the length desired by the practitioner. Given the size of the list provided above as an example, it is still possible to use it for the day's calendar (for example) since each number can represent an hour session in a working day. So having a few short lists that are there to serve such a purpose is reasonable- in which case extending all lists is not necessary- some should be short and some long in order to correspond to the different types of data needed to be memorised.

Alphabet list

Much like the number list serves both as a unique identifier for each number as well as a peg list, the alphabet list serves dual purposes too, these are listed as follows:

1. It provides a unique image to represent each letter- this is useful when memorising abstract ideas that involve letter in an otherwise illogical manner (alphabetically speaking)- for example in mathematical formulae as shown later in the section.
2. The list, given that the letters have a natural numerical order, can also serve as a peg list.

It is simple to remember this list, as with other peg lists, as the underlying elements that form the list have a logical aspect or rule that connects them. In the case of the numbers' list it was the use of the phonetic alphabet, in the case of the effigy list it was the shape of the number and here in the alphabet list it is the most colourful image that sounds like the letter:

Letter	Peg
A	Ape
B	Bee
C	Sea
D	Dill
E	Eel
F	Elf
G	Jin
H	Hedge
I	Eye
J	Jail
K	Cane
L	Hell
M	Ham
N	Hen
O	Ho Ho Ho (Santa)
P	Pea
Q	Cue
R	RRR (think pirate)
S	Ace
T	Tea
U	Hugh (think Hugh Grant)
V	Veal
W	W (think George Bush)
X	Eggs
Y	Wine
Z	Zit

Rhyme list

The following list was derived by finding a word for an object that rhymes with the number:

Number	Peg
0	Zorro
1	Gun
2	Zoo
3	Tree
4	Door
5	Hive
6	Vicks
7	Heaven
8	Slate
9	Mine
10	Zen (think Buddhist monk)

Body list

The list below uses body parts registered from the head downwards; this list does not immediately provide a numerical reference point but it can be added by remembering which are the 5th, 10th, 15th ...etc points in the list- for example, the Tongue is the 5th item on the list and the stomach is the 10th items whilst the toes are the 15th item- this is easy to remember as each belong to a different section of the body (tongue is in upper third, stomach in middle third and toes in lower third).

Body Part
Head
Eyes
Nose
Mouth
Tongue
Neck
Chest
Arms
Fingers
Stomach
Groin
Thighs
Calves
Foot
Toes

When new information is pegged to the list, if a numerical position is required it is simple to work it out from one of the markers created. For example, say that the item pegged to Mouth was a mosquito- it would be simple to work out that mosquito is the fourth item in the list since Tongue is number 5.

Loci system

The loci system is treated separately even though it is a form of a peg list. The crucial distinction is that the loci system relies on a memory of a place be it a city, a house, a room a road etc. The location does not have to be created artificially like the lists we have presented above; instead, the location should be somewhere extremely familiar to you and it should contain lots of visual object, items or monuments that can be used as places to deposit information. This system allows for storage of an incredibly large amount of data which is only limited by the size of the location. The information can be stored as fast as one takes to mentally move around the space that the location brings to mind. The other advantage of this system is that the topic being memorised can be self-contained in the location chosen; this means that revision of the topic can be done without notes since all it entails is walking through the aforementioned location (walking through mentally) and reviewing the pegs created along the way.

In order to use this method with the ability to also recall the numerical position of the item, markers will have to be placed in key increments along the way (as presented in the body list).

Houses and Rooms

A classic example would be to take a room in your house and work clockwise recording all the items that can be used as fixed objects to which information can be attached. The requirements are as follows:

1. Work clockwise through every room.
2. Work clockwise around the house, going from lowest to highest floor.
3. Perform the journey (mentally) a few times before attaching any items, during these journeys record in your mind which items you will use according to the following criteria:

a. The items should be fixed to the location in the room (e.g Fridge or Oven) or at least the place where they are deposited is always the same.

b. The items are distinct and easy to visualise.

c. Avoid using the same type of items several times in each room (for example, using several books would not be good whilst using the whole bookcase would be much better).

4. If numerical order is desired, place a marker every 5 items- for example you may choose to use an association that would signify the number, e.g. putting a rail next to the 45th item in a very absurd manner would be a good marker. The reader should note that this is not necessary if numerical order is not important for the memory task, or if every 5 items is too granular; you may choose to instead place a marker every 100 items or no marker at all- it all depends on the intended use of the loci. One may choose to have some loci with markers as well as others without- the former can then be applied for memory tasks that required numeric positioning whilst the latter can be used for everything else.

5. Once established, review the journey in your mind a few times to ensure it is fixed- you can extend a journey but **do not change or alter what has already been established.**

For example, take a room in your house, say the kitchen; going clockwise you notice:

Fridge, microwave, toaster, sink, oven, cupboard, bin, a blender etc...

You now have a list to which new information can be attached- for example you may decide that you would use your house, going clockwise through each room, clockwise around the house from the bottom up, in order to memorise the list of presidents of the United States. Using the example room above (and assuming it is the first room in the house) we would peg George Washington to the fridge,

John Adams to the Microwave, Thomas Jefferson to the toaster and so on. The issue of converting the name into a picture would be clarified in the applications section, the only point that should be understood in this section is that all we are doing here is using a location which is known in our mind in order store information which was previously unknown.

Note that as with all memory techniques, the glue for connecting the unknown item to the known item on the loci is the same- use absurd images and ludicrous actions as discussed in previous sections.

Palaces, cities and countries

To remember longer lists of items or larger topics, one would require a larger location than household rooms. The principle remains the same, all that is needed is to have locations that are already known and clear in the mind, then apply the same technique as for the room of the house. The key is to be systematic, the journey must be the same, so for example say you would like to use your journey to work as the loci; the most important point is to always follow the monuments along the journey in the same way you encounter them and not to change the order as it suits you. If the order is changed, the method still works but the ability to recall sequences is diminished as well as the ability to orderly travel along the topic as it was memorised on the loci. This is of greater concern when the practitioner uses a city as the loci; here one is able to travel the city using different routes and side streets which would not be in accordance with the rules of this system. The practitioner is therefore recommended to follow one route that systematically passes through all the streets and side alleys- one approach could be to start at the south and work towards the north in a systematic east to west sweep- from above it would seem like a snake crawling north. This works well for any type of city or loci, be it a round structure or square. Another approach that can be taken for round loci is to travel in circles either from the inside out or the outside in.

The preferred method remains to be the choice of the practitioner, the key rules are:

1. Travel along the loci chosen via the same route, do not change or improvise along the way.
2. Cover the territory by following an efficient travel route that covers the entire loci- thus using up most of what it has to offer.
3. Choose the monuments along the way and after that, do not change them.
4. Peg the information being studied to the monuments along the way (using absurd images and nonsensical action as before).
5. Review by mentally travelling along the chosen journey across your loci.

Some examples of what can be used:

1. Palaces- if you have had the pleasure to roam through a palace or have seen a documentary of such a journey, this makes good loci.
2. Museums- with all the artefacts along the way this represents an excellent choice of loci.
3. Art galleries.
4. Journey to work.
5. Journey to a friend.
6. Neighbourhood you grew up in or the one in which you currently reside.
7. Village.
8. Town or city.
9. Country.

The above list is ordered by level of difficulty; it is simple to walk through a palace or a museum and become familiar with the items along the way and then use these with the system discussed.

However, once we consider whole cities and countries it becomes much more difficult since the necessary loci has to first be mapped out in the mind.

For most purposes, the need to have a whole town as one's loci is superfluous- this is usually reserved for the memorisation of very large chunks of information in competitive situations (for example memorising as many decks of cards possible is one of the challenges in the world memory championships). However, the ability to map out in one's mind a whole city/town is not impossible and can in fact be very fun to do. All that is needed is the desire to go for a walk (or ride a bike) systematically through the desired location and enjoy the scenery whilst noting any monuments that can become useful pegs. This is just sightseeing and it is something most of the population perform as a leisure activity- doing more of this fun activity would provide more storage space for other bits of data. The approach could be one of the following:

1. Go sightseeing (museums, towns, cities etc) and note the monuments that are of interest to you. Be systematic in the way you cover the territory taking brief notes (writing down, taking a photo or a video) along the way for future reference if necessary.

2. Have a topic that you wish to memorise and take it with you on a journey. At each monument you encounter attempt to memorise a new bit of information from your topic by pegging it to the monument you see in front of you. Again, proceed systematically through the territory to ensure an orderly coverage.

3. Once you complete either of the two approaches above, mentally review your journey a few times, noting the monuments along the way. Once you are comfortable with the journey and the monuments along the way do not change them.

An example of loci could be as follow (using the route taken to go to work):

1. Entrance to the **building** in which the practitioner resides.
2. Traversing the road at the **zebra crossing.**
3. Walking past an **old pub** with the blue sign (names of monuments are not important it is the visual representation that matters).
4. Crossing the **bridge** to enter the wharf.
5. Passing by the **ferry station.**
6. Saying good morning to the favourite waiter at the **Chinese restaurant** that is next to the large **flight of stairs.**
7. To the left is the **Four Seasons hotel.**
8. Continuing straight, entering **a circular garden.**
9. Past the **garden** and onto to the **main road.**
10. Crossing the street standing in front a **high rise building** made from glass and steel.

The above is a simple example, the key is to create your own journey- one you have experienced and can recall well. Once you practise this method, you would come to appreciate its power; the enjoyable feeling of mentally re-visiting pleasant sceneries at the same time as revising a topic is priceless and makes studying that much more enjoyable.

Imaginary places

This technique is an extension of the loci system that uses one's creative powers to build loci mentally. The idea is to simply relax and mentally construct a house, palace, town, city, country or world- it is much like the SimCity computer game, the only difference is that you are not limited by the variations that the computer allows- you are only limited by your imagination- which for all intents and purposes is infinite.

This method is more difficult to apply since the new creations have to become familiar before they can be used as loci. Vivid location building is crucial and requires some practise for mastery.

When one physically visits a location, the memory of the scenery is automatic and vivid but when one creates something in the mind which does not exist, the memory requires more effort to stick. With practise, this can become automatic- the practitioner is recommended to experiment with this technique.

A simple example could be to create a neighbourhood for the purpose of grouping together and memorising all books of a certain genre. For example, say you wanted to memorise a group of 10 leadership books you recently read, the procedure would be as follows:

1. Create a small neighbourhood.
2. Build a road, visualise the colour of the road the width of the pavement the trees along the way etc.
3. Visualise a "leading" book with military uniform and a sword, see how he is leading the army of books that is marching behind him- vividly picture the billions of books marching to this leader's commands on the new road you have just created.
4. Now build a house at the entrance to your road, give this house a post box and peg the name of the book being memorised to the post box. It could for example be Sun Tzu's "The art of War", you would then picture a post box that is at war with a canvass (to remind you of art) - picture the two warring using machine guns and tanks- i.e. make ludicrous vivid images pegging the two items.
5. Next, walk on the footpath leading to the house- vividly picture the house, create it in any way you wish: modern, western, eastern, new, old, large, small, what colour is the main door? What colour is the house painted in? Etc...

6. When you enter the house, what is the first room you walk into? Is it the living room? If so, what is in it? What colour is it? Once the first room has been created, work your way clockwise through the items in the room and peg to each item one key point from the first chapter of the book (remember to use exaggerated ludicrous imagery).

7. Proceed with the rest of the rooms- each room corresponds to a chapter.

8. Exit the house and walk to the next house on your road- it can be on the opposite side or it could be that the houses are all on one side of the road, with perhaps a view towards the sea on the other side- the choice is yours, build it as you wish.

9. Give this house a different post box or no box at all, you can create a variation here where you peg the name of the book with the footpath leading to the house instead of using the post box- it is up to you, the possibilities are infinite. You can even make the colour of the house to be in the pattern with which the front cover of the book is painted.

10. Enter the second house and allocate each room to a chapter memorising key points by pegging each bit of information being memorised to one item in the room.

Extensions:

a. Once you have created a road you can connect it to the next road which may, for example, store books you have read about history where each house corresponds to a different era being memorised.

b. Once your neighbourhood is created you can place a major road connecting it to the next neighbourhood- until a city has been established.

c. Then proceed by creating more cities, then countries, then worlds etc.

The reader is advised to regularly visit these locations and to walk through them (mentally of course) so that the information is reviewed and eventually stored in the long term memory banks (refer to the section about reviewing and repetition in order to find the optimal times to perform this).

It is fascinating to lie down on your bed, or even better in a hammock between two trees, and mentally walk through the imaginary universes you have created. It is very gratifying, enhances creativity, improves spatial awareness and, above all, it facilitates storage of vast amounts of information.

The grid system

The grid system is primarily used to memorise visual data and the shape with which the data is presented. It can also be used as a standard peg list but, since peg lists are easier to derive, the grid is most often used for its visual applications.

A typical example would be to memorise a map, card arrangements, a graph or the periodic table. A modification of the grid method into a circular representation also allows adaptation into rotund type of objects- the world map (elliptic) or a maze for example.

The approach taken to memorise items using the grid is exactly the same as the method used for the peg and loci systems- simply peg the new item to the item that represents its position on the grid (see examples below).

The standard grid

The standard grid is the main tool which can be used to capture any visual two-dimensional data. The procedure for the creation of the grid is as follows:

1. Draw the grid.
2. Input letters on the first row and numbers in the first column.
3. Each cell is named using the letter first and then the number.
4. The unique image for each cell is created by finding a word that begins with the corresponding letter and has the phonetic sounds as re-presented by the number (see the phonetic alphabet section- remember it is only the sound that matters in the phonetic alphabet, not the letters).
5. Ensure the words are unique and do not change them once established.
6. Increase the grid size if required by adding rows and columns.

Provided below is an example of a 5x5 grid created according to the above procedure:

	A	B	C	D	E
1	Ad (think of a funny tv ad you know)	Bat	Cod	Dodo	Eddie (Frasier's dog)
2	Annoy (visualise someone banging a spoon on a pot)	Bono (U2 singer)	Can	Dean	Eon (visualise a sandglass)
3	Ammo	Beam	Comb	Dam	Emmy (picture the Emmy award)
4	Air	Bar	Crow	Dry (think of hair dryer)	Ear
5	Ali (visualise Muhammad Ali)	Ball	Clay	Doll	El (think of El Niño)

This grid can be extended across columns or rows or both; the key is to have a unique identifier for each point on the grid.

A classic example demonstrating an application of this system is to memorise the elements in the periodic table as well as its structure. In the example below, we will only include the first 25 elements but the extension to the entire table can be performed by simply using a larger grid:

	A	B	C	D	E
1	Hydrogen				
2	Lithium	Beryllium			
3	Sodium	Magnesium			
4	Potassium	Calcium	Scandium	Titanium	Vanadium
5	Rubidium	Strontium	Yttrium	Zirconium	Niobium

In order to memorise the portion of the periodic table presented above it is only necessary to peg each item in the periodic table to the corresponding object that represents its position in the standard grid. For example, Lithium is in A2 and so to remember its position in the table one could simply visualise an annoying lithium battery banging on a pot annoying all those around it (hear the noise and feel the discomfort in the scene). Another example could be Vanadium which is in E4- the image for this grid point is ear- perhaps visualise Jean-Claude Van Damme (Van Damme to remember Vanadium) in a street fight, trying to high kick a gigantic muscular ear.

To then remember the atomic number of each element there are two options:

1. After pegging the element to its position on the table, link the atomic number to the element. In the example for Vanadium, perhaps link Van Damme to a gnome (Atomic number = 23 which is represented by a gnome).
2. Or, if the entire table has been memorised, the atomic number can be worked out by finding the position in the table- i.e. counting the number of steps (travelling horizontally and from top to bottom) from a known element. For example if you know that calcium has an atomic number of 20, it is simple to work out that Titanium would have an atomic number of 22.

The first approach is preferable as it allows a quicker recall of the necessary information.

The numerical grid

In a similar way to the standard grid, the numerical grid is created using the following procedure:

1. Draw the grid.
2. Input numbers on the first row and numbers in the first column.
3. Each cell is named using the phonetic letters of the column first and then the row.
4. Ensure the words are unique and do not change them once established.
5. Increase the grid size if required by adding rows and columns.

	1	2	3
1	Tot	Knot	Mat
2	Ton	Neon	Man
3	Dame	Anime	Mime

The application approach is precisely the same as for the standard grid.

The Circular grid

The approach to the circular grid is exactly the same as for the rectangular grid; each sector is represented by a letter first and then a number. The circles are growing outward, so A is the inner most circle, B is the next and it encompasses A- and so on for C, D...etc.

The numbers are allocated clockwise beginning with one from the top vertical point.

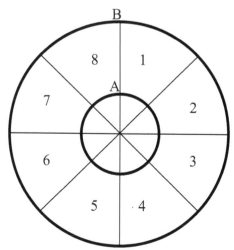

The naming convention is the same per the rectangular grid- for example, the first sector in the A circle is A1 which would be represented by Ad. The final sector in the B circle is represented by B8 and the image would be beef.

An application example could be London's inner boroughs; imposing this map onto our circular grid would look like the following:

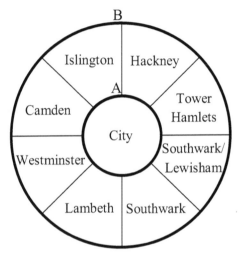

To memorise simply peg each borough's name to the sector it is in. For example Hackney is in B1- this could be visualised by seeing a Bat with a Hacked Knee- visualise this poor bat limping with pain in its gigantic Knee which has been partially hacked off. Another example could be sector B8 which is represented by the word beef- see a juicy beef steak walking through a Grizzly-town (for Islington)- feel the fear this steak must be experiencing as he begins to accept his inevitable fate.

Note that the inner (A) circle did not need to be broken down into circle since the entire circle represents "City"- to remember this simply peg the image for this letter (Ape) to the borough (City) - perhaps visualise a city of apes instead of people- imagine boarding the underground at Leicester square only to realise it is filled with Apes on their journey to work, busy reading their morning papers. [No offense intended to any City dwellers]

It is simple to extend the circular method by including more circles, simply add another circle on the outside and extend the diameter lines outward.

A modification of this method is to use more sectors so that the circle is divided into 12 pieces, which corresponds to a clock type decomposition of the circle.

This method can be used to memorise circular cities, circular maps, mazes, pie-charts, planets etc. The procedure is exactly the same as for the rectangular grids:

1. Simply superimpose the grid onto the information that needs to be memorised.
2. Figure out what information resides in each sector.
3. Peg the information in the sector with the image that represents the sector.

Another modification of the circular grid is to use a numerical approach, so instead of each circle being represented by a letter it is represented by a number. This is analogous to the numerical grid approach.

Empty spaces and data that stretches over several grid-points

A note regarding empty spaces and repeated data is in order; for example, in the periodic table above, B1 to E1 were empty- usually familiarity with the topic would allow the practitioner to know this feature when recalling. However, to improve confidence in the technique, it is always possible to memorise the grid points that are empty by pegging them to a baseball players' bench (since those sitting on the bench are not playing, in much the same way as empty spaces are not relevant). For example, we could peg to the bench the image for B1- visualising lots of bats sitting on the bench looking onto the field eagerly waiting for their turn to play. Then continue by linking C1 to B1, C1 to D1 etc. Or, if everything is empty between B1 and E1- instead of linking each individual grid point that is empty, one can simply bundle the start and end into one image to remind that the whole section is empty- in this case, the image would be lots of bat shaped creatures with Eddie's head waiting to go on the pitch.

The overall procedure is:

1. Visualise the baseball bench.
2. Peg the first empty grid point image to the bench.
3. Link the next empty grid point image to the previous empty grid point's image.
4. Or, if a whole sector is empty, create one image by bundling the start and the end point images into one image and link to the bench. Then proceed by linking the next empty sector's image to the previous empty sector's image.

For grid points that contain data that is present in another grid point, as for example in the London map where B3 and B4 both have Southwark- simply link each grid point image to Southwark independently as you would any other grid point. However, if a very large sector contains a repeated item (for example the oceans in a map of the world would take up large sectors of grid points), simply bundle the start and end grid points of the item and peg the image of the item to this bundle's image.

Note that one does not need to stick to rows only or columns only. For example in the periodic table, C1 to E3 are empty- this rectangle sector covers most of the empty points and should therefore be bundled up to create the image that should be pegged to the bench. Similarly this can be applied in the case of a repeated item, like the ocean in the world map example.

Applications

The best way to complete the exposition of a topic is by providing examples of how it can be incorporated in daily lives and practical use. The examples that were provided for each system should have served the purpose of explaining the general approach; the sections below should serve to reinforce the concepts as well as to emphasise the key rules of how the memorisation of every topic should be approached.

The purpose of this section is also to illustrate how different techniques should be used under different circumstances and which technique is optimal for each type of information. The reader should note that the choices assigned here are based on the author's experience; these choices have been made based on performance that was measured in terms of speed of memorisation, speed of recall as well as accuracy achieved. After mastery of the techniques, the practitioner may choose to vary the systems used across topics in a different order than the ones presented below- it is advisable to verify the improvement achieved before doing so permanently.

Foreign Vocabulary

With the application of the **link system**, learning foreign vocabulary is simple, fun and effortless. The procedure is as follows:

1. Convert the foreign word into something that can be visualised.
2. Convert the translation into something that can be visualised.
3. Link the two using a ludicrous image and absurd actions.
4. Review by testing yourself immediately after memorising, then at the following intervals: after- 1hour, 12 hours, 24

hours, 1 week, 2 weeks, 1 month, 3 months, 6 months, 12 months.

Mandarin Chinese:

Ying Hung - a bank

Picture an inkwell (the vessel used to store ink for fountain pens) being hung in the middle of the bank by a very violent and menacing bank clerk, perhaps because the inkwell has taken an unauthorised overdraft. Picture the scene vividly, with the noose being tightened around the inkwell and the fear in its eyes. Visualise the scene in your bank or your typical idea of what a bank looks like on the inside- it could be in a vault full of gold for example and the inkwell is trying to place its foot on one of the stacks of gold or money to avoid being strangled by the rope.

Fung Chien – the room

Picture a hotel room that is being occupied by a chain that is made out of fungus links instead of metal links. Visualise the fungus chain jumping out of the double bed and into the hotel slippers making its way to the en suite bathroom to wash its face. As always, exaggerate the image- visualise that the fungus chain is enormous and when it is lying in the bed its lower links are bulging out and when it gets out of bed the whole room shakes and all other hotel guests are shouting for it to quiet down.

A crucial note is due at this point; an optimal application of the technique would be to use the same images when breaking down similar sounding sounds in other words. For example, in Chinese, key syllables can be used in several permutations within a word- each meaning a completely different thing. The general approach should then be:

1. If the whole foreign word sounds similar to an easily visualised object then convert it that way.
2. Otherwise, break the word down into key sounds and convert these into similarly sounding objects.
3. When new words are encountered, break the sounds in a consistent way; so from the example above, whenever "Ying" is encountered in any new Chinese word that you learn, make sure you use the image of an inkwell. It is strongly advisable to use a notebook to ensure key sounds are defined and applied consistently (i.e. create a list of unique identifiers).

Japanese

Chumon – to order

Picture a patron in a restaurant chewing on a moon and raising his hand to order more food; visualise the gigantic moon in this human's mouth and his attempts at chewing it down into palatable pieces, but he is so hungry he wants to order more such moons.

French

Colère – anger

Picture a dog's collar that is getting angry at the owner for pulling on him the whole day. Visualise the large and scary collar getting angry and turning redder, with steam emanating from its top- see the owner cowering in fear from this gigantic monster that he has unleashed.

Arabic

Tabeeb – a doctor

Picture the hip of a tab (as in the bill) being damaged and the tab limping slowly towards the doctor's clinic- there the doctor inspects the hip and writes the tab a prescription for the pain. Visualise absurdity of the tab having a hip and how the doctor is examining the hip with care as it would for any other human. Exaggerate the sizes and feel the pain the tab must be going through.

Spanish

Sellos (pronounced selyos) – stamps

Picture a lady looking at herself in the mirror and being terrified by the cellulose on the back of her thighs. She is shocked to find that, as she has aged, she has developed horrendous looking cellulite that look like gigantic stamps of different countries. Clearly see the back of her thighs with the massive stamps that connect the skin and sense the shock she is experiencing.

Integration into daily life

If you are in the process of learning a new language, or always wanted to do so, go and buy a popular study course and work through the lessons as recommended therewith. When new words are encountered, use the system above to memorise them; it is advisable to write the new words down in a notebook and to note down the images used, for future reference if required. This notebook can then be used for the review of the material in the optimal times suggested above. Each entry in the notebook should carry the following information:

a. The foreign word followed by a hyphen.
b. After the hyphen, write down the translation.
c. Next to the translation enter square brackets in which you enter the image for the foreign word.
d. Next to the image of the foreign word enter a hyphen followed by the image of the translation, and close the brackets.
e. It is preferable to use black ink for the information and green ink for the images

f.   e.g.
Ying Hung - a bank [ink hung - a bank]
Fung Chien – the room [fungus chain - a room]

Non-Foreign Vocabulary

The same techniques used for foreign vocabulary can be used for non-foreign vocabulary; the procedure stays the same- examples below illustrate the principles:

Pejorative – A word expressing contempt or disapproval

Picture a rat driving a Peugeot: as he slows down next to the garden of Eden to speak to Eve, he rolls down the window and begins to express his contempt for her behaviour with Adam- vividly see the large rat in the Peugeot shaking his head in disapproval whilst Eve is looking down in shame. Exaggerate the image, and sense the feelings being expressed.

Hegemony – Leadership or dominance, esp. by one country or social group over others

Picture a hedge made out money leading an army of smaller hedges into war; vividly see the monetary bills that grow on the branches of the leading hedge and sense the atmosphere as the leader is gathering his hedge troops to war.

Integration into daily life

As with foreign vocabulary, the procedure with non-foreign words is the same. A simple approach could be to put in a notebook any word that you come across during the day whose meaning you do not know. This could be words seen or heard on the radio, TV, newspaper, book, and magazine or in conversation. Put all these

words in a notebook in the following format and review at the
optimal intervals as instructed in previous sections:

a. The new word followed by a hyphen.
b. After the hyphen write down the meaning.
c. Next to the meaning enter square brackets in which you enter
    the image for the new word.
d. Next to the image of the new word enter a hyphen followed
    by the image of the meaning, and close the brackets.
e. It is preferable to use black ink for the information and green
    ink for the images
f. e.g.
    Pejorative - disapproval [Peugeot/rat/eve – "dissing" and
    shaking head from side to side]
    Hegemony - Leadership [Hedge/Money– Leading an army
    into war]

Spelling

The spelling of words that have a challenging and confusing
combination of letters that appear to have little logic when compared
to the pronunciation of similar sounding tones; those spelling can
easily be remembered by applying the alphabet list of words
presented earlier in this section. This list converts each letter into a
unique picture which can then be used to remind the user which
letters feature in the spelling of the word, and thus remove the
confusion. The procedure is as follows:

1. Create an image for the word whose spelling is being
    considered.
2. Create an image for the problematic combination of letters.
3. Link the two in an absurd manner.

4. For a combination of repeated letters for which we do not have an image, create a unique identifier, for example:

"**cc**" - syringe (cc being the unit of measurement on a syringe).
"**ss**" - Nazi (ss common name for the Schutzstaffel which was a paramilitary organisation under the Nazi party).
"**ll**" - LL cool J (the rapper).
"**mm**"- Road runner (the cartoon character always says "Meep Meep" before speeding away from Coyote.

An example:

Necessary – the spelling of this word is often confused with "Neccesary" or "Neccessary". To remember that there is only one "c" and two "s" we create the following image:

Visualise a NASA astronaut wearing a Sari (Nasa-Sari) instead of a space suit whilst walking on the moon. He then jumps into a sea of Nazis and begins to swim to the other side, but these violent Nazis are attempting to kill him for wearing a Sari- feel the fear he must be experiencing and the hate displayed towards him. Exaggerate everything, see the sea as a collection of billions or even trillions of Nazi soldiers, and clearly see the splash caused as the astronaut jumps in.

It is now simple to recall that the word necessary is spelled with one "c" and two "s". To some readers necessary may have been an apt example, whilst to others it may appear as a trivial one. The key is that this technique can be used on any word and any spelling combinations.

Telephone numbers

This technique uses the 1-100 number list created earlier in this section. The procedure is as follows:

1. Create an image for the person or company to whom the number belongs.
2. Create an image (or a series of images) for the telephone number.
3. Link the image of the person or company to the first image for the phone number.
4. Then link the first image of the phone number to the rest.

Examples (note that the numbers below are not real for obvious reasons):

555-3495 – Flower shop

Flower shop is simple to visualise, so proceed with breaking down the number into images: Lily, Lamb, Rib and Lee. Proceed by picturing a flower shop where the shop assistant is a gigantic Lily. Next visualise a lamb whose wool is made out of Lilies. Then picture a lamb sitting at a table and eating human ribs; next visualise a rib practising the nunchakus whilst yelling menacing warrior's cries.

+44-666-6219 - Nigel

Say you would like to memorise the phone number that belongs to a friend who lives in the UK. If you know that the UK country code is 44 then there is no need to add it on to your picture, simply proceed with the rest. The aim should be to only memorise all that is unknown. Therefore, in this example, you can proceed to 666- here we can make use of a simple association that uniquely identifies the number 666 with an image- namely the devil. So picture the devil smearing Nike Gel (to represent Nigel) over himself before entering the hot climates of hell. Then picture a devil appearing on the shoulder of a chain and whispering in its ear, advising it to do an evil deed. Continue by picturing toilet paper roll that is made out of large metallic chains rather than paper (feel the discomfort).

Note that, if the reader chooses to use the higher dimensional approach (for example adding 2 dimensions), the images would be as follows: Nike gel to Devil and Devil to a Red Chain that is exploding (using the convention VWYZ). Therefore here, one could picture a red chain that is made out of devils and it increases in size until it explodes.

Whatever approach taken, be consistent- for example if the high dimensional approach is taken, it is important to decide which dimensional convention is being used for which portion of the number, and to continue to use this approach without exceptions or changes.

The reader is advised to practise with phone numbers as encountered during the day. Practise by attempting to recall mentally, before accessing the number from the cellular device or rolodex. With practise you will gain confidence and mastery.

Cards

To memorise cards, we require a systematic conversion of each element in a pack of cards into a visual object. The simplest approach is to use our list of 1-100 numbers with the following rules:

Numbers	Suit
1 to 13	Spades
21 to 33	Hearts
41 to 53	Clubs
61 to 73	Diamonds

This approach assigns a unique image to each card in the deck. The convention used is that 1 is equal to Ace, the numbers 2-10 as they are, 11 is Jack, 12 is Queen and 13 is King. For example Jack of Clubs would be number 51 and would be represented by "Latte". 5 of Diamonds would be number 65 and would be represented by "Jail".

Memorising a deck of cards is now a simple matter; we use the loci method to allow us to capture the sequence with the order in which it was memorised. For example, let us use an example of a journey that has the following monuments along the way:

Bar, Church, Gym, Bridge, Shoe shop

Say the sequence in the pack is as follows:

10 of Diamonds, Jack of Clubs, Queen of diamonds, King of clubs, Ace of spades

This sequence would be represented by the numbers 70, 51, 72, 53, 1 and the corresponding images would be: Case, Latte, Coin, Lamb, and Tie.

To memorise the sequence, peg Case to Bar, for example picture a gigantic Briefcase walking through the swinging door of the bar, everyone in the bar stops what they are doing, the music pauses as the Briefcase slowly walks to the bar.

Next peg Latte to Church, visualise a hot Latte standing in the entrance to the Church, dressed in preacher's clothes urging you to come in and repent your sins.

Continue by pegging Coin to Gym, Lamb to Bridge and Tie to Shoe shop. Walk through the journey a few times vividly seeing the pegs created along the way. In order to recall the sequence, all that is required is to walk again through the journey and the pegs will provide the details of the card sequence memorised.

In order to memorise a longer sequence of cards (hundreds or thousands), the practitioner would need a journey that contains as many items. It is simple to create such sequences and it is useful to always have at least 2 sequences with at least 100 items in each. However, for memory championships, one would require journeys that consist of large portions of towns or cities to allow for pegging of thousands of images.

To reduce the need for longer lists, it is always possible to use higher dimensional images taking in the information of 2 or more cards at a time. For example we could use the "VWYZ" convention (VW=number from the list of 1-100 numbers, Y=colour dimension, Z=action dimension) to capture two cards in each image by making two cards represent one number. From the example above, this would mean taking the 10 of diamonds and the Jack of clubs together to stand for 7051, and the image to represent this number is an "orange briefcase that is having a shower"- so we would peg this image to the bar, which is the first point on our journey- perhaps you walk into a bar and see that there is an "orange briefcase that is having a shower" in the middle of the room.

Using higher dimensions reduces the required length of the journey since more information is being attached to each point on the journey. This is very powerful and with practise it can give the practitioner a serious edge over other competitors. The obvious extension would be to expand the number list from 1-100 to 1-9,999 and then add 4 dimensions which would provide the ability to put 4 cards on each point in the journey.

The reader should note that practise is required to make the process of translating the cards into numbers, then into images and then to quickly peg these images to the journey, in very short periods of time. When adding dimensions it is usually the speed of translating into numbers that tends to suffer- but with practise it can be made almost automatic.

Binary code

Sequences of binary digits can be easily memorised using the loci method. Again we provide unique identifiers for each combination and place it along the journey in absurd ways. The unique identifiers up to second order are presented below:

Numbers	Image
00	Toilet
11	Date (the fruit)
01	Suit
10	Toes

For example using the same journey as before (Bar, Church, Gym, Bridge, Shoe shop), memorise the following binary sequence: 0111010100

Simply peg Suit to Bar, Date to Church, Suit to Gym, Suit to Bridge and Toilet to Shoe shop.

As before, extension with higher dimensions would reduce the number of images required.

Another approach to improve the technique would be to create a higher order list of unique identifiers; the table above is only of second order. With fourth order, a list of all the binary permutations of "XXXX" would have to be mapped out (e.g. 0000, 0101, 0111, 1000 etc...) with a unique identifier assigned to each. Using a fourth order list would mean that the sequence is being memorised in chunks of 4 digits at a time. It is then also possible to add dimensions to make the chunks bigger still- for example by adding colour and action dimensions, each image would represent 6 digits.

It is simple to notice why the loci system was chosen for this task; say one tried to use the link system instead- for a long sequence this would likely result in errors as the images begin to repeat themselves. In a journey this is irrelevant, since even if the same digits repeat many times, they are linked along a journey on which their presence would be registered as unusual, and their recall at that point on the journey cannot be confused with an earlier point since the journey is unique and already known.

Computer code

As with all other applications, we need to breakdown the subject into key components and provide unique identifiers for each. Since computer languages vary substantially, we will provide a prototypical example based on C++ code from which the reader can easily adapt to other languages.

As always we begin with unique identifiers:

Component	Image
int	Inn (picture a small motel)
main	Menu
()	Twin Towers
{	Spider
}	Spider
Cout	Axe (as cout sounds like cut)
<<	Pacman
\	Slide
,	Comatose
"	Snake (as it looks like a snake bite)
return	An urn full of rats
;	A winking eye

Using these identifiers, we can memorise the following code using the link system:

----

int main()

{

      cout << "Hello, World!\n"

      return 0;

}

Begin by linking the name of the program "Hello World" with the code- in this case we would link the image of a world waving hello to a small motel, then we see an image of a large restaurant menu checking into a motel with his girlfriend, the next image is that of the two motels being built horizontally in the form of the twin towers, then see the image of a large spider that has twin towers for legs, then see a spider that is cutting trees in the forest with an enormous axe, then see Pacman being cut down with an axe, then proceed to Pacman biting a snake viscously, then proceed to visualising a phone (hello) that is made out of a gigantic snake, proceed to a phone lying connected to a life support machine (because it is comatose) then picture a world, with lots of unhealthy looking exclamation marks all over him ,lying connected to a life support machine, proceed to seeing a young world sliding down a water slide yelling with joy, then picture a hen sliding down the water slides getting all the feathers wet feeling very confused, proceed by seeing a large group of hens with snakes instead of pecks, then picture a snake drinking from an urn full of rats, proceed to an urn full of rats running down the street with a chainsaw like a madman attacking all that lays in its path, proceed by seeing an eye walking down the aisle of a hardware store winking at the massive chainsaw on display who returns a smile, finally visualise a spider that has a twitch and his eye keeps winking at his pray.

The worked example focused on breaking down the code into small components. However, as one becomes familiar with computer code, the general rules of the particular language means that you would know (in the example of C++) that each beginning "{" should end with "}" similarly each " would be followed by " at the end of a string. Knowing the key rules of a language means that all that needs to be memorised is the code rather than the overall structure. The key principles are the same, just stick to unique identifiers at the granularity you desire.

Experienced programmers will not need to memorise the sequence of a code since this can be generated from knowledge of the logic required for a particular program. Instead they may use the technique to memorise the name of the function, the inputs required and what the function does. Advanced use of computer code generally focuses on calling other functions throughout the code- having a vast mental database of functions speeds up code writing considerably.

Mathematical formulae

The link system is used in order to memorise mathematical formulae; the procedure, as always, requires a unique representation of each element, for the example below we will use the following table:

Symbol	Image	Why
+	Pus	Plus sounds like Pus
-	Dennis the Menace	Minus sounds like Menace
=	Eagle	Equal sounds like Eagle
2π	Two pies	Since the letter is pi and there are two
μ	A cow	Since the letter is pronounced mu
$\sqrt{}$	Root	Since it is the square root symbol
( )	Twin Towers	Since visually it looks like two towers
σ	Sigmund Freud	Since the letter is pronounced Sigma
Division	Machete	Division is associated with cutting...
Power	Bodybuilder	Power associated with muscles
Integration	Interrogation light	Integration sounds like interrogation
Differentiation	Sock	Differentiating between the pairs of socks

The reader may be daunted by the size of the table required to memorise a shorter looking formula; however, it should be noted that the table is built in order to form a unique and consistent approach which will be applied to all formulae ever memorised- without using a table certain duplications or inconsistent naming conventions may be applied in the future, which could lead to confusion and inaccurate recall. It requires only a small effort to maintain a table of unique identifiers but the rewards are a more systematic approach and thus better recall.

To demonstrate the application to mathematical formulae, let us memorise the equation for the normal distribution density function. The procedure is as follows:

1. Create a unique set of identifiers for each element.
2. Link the name of the equation to the first element in the equation.
3. Proceed by connecting the rest of the elements using the link method
    a. Go from left to right,
    b. Up to down.
4. Review.

Taking the formula below as the example:

$$f(x) = \frac{1}{\sigma\sqrt{2\pi}} e^{-\frac{(\mu-x)^2}{2\sigma^2}}$$

Since we have already created a unique set of identifiers (letters will be presented by the images from the alphabet list whilst symbols will use images from the table above) we proceed by converting the name of the equation into an image- for a normal distribution think of wide bell (since the distribution looks like a bell), now link this wide bell to the first element which is an elf, imagine a little elf ringing the gigantic wide golden bell to alert everyone that dinner is ready, proceed to linking an elf to an egg that is being crushed between two towers- perhaps as the egg breaks out comes an elf, then link the egg being crushed by the two towers with an eagle, perhaps this is all happening in the eagle's nest and he is asking them to stop, continue by linking the eagle to a tie that is being cut with a machete by a white beard (Sigmund Freud)- imagine the eagle trying to pull at the tie to save it's life as the vicious white beard is cutting it, then link the white beard to two pies that are made out of roots- perhaps the beard is tasting the two pies and is disgusted by the "rooty" taste, then link the eel to the two rooty ties- perhaps the two pies are electrified by the eel and their roots are set on fire, proceed by linking a massive bodybuilder Dennis the menace (bodybuilder since it is to the power) that has gigantic eels instead of biceps, then proceed by visualising Dennis riding a tower that is made out of cow's skin, then link Dennis that has a gigantic egg head and is trying to eat the tower that is made out of cow's skin, continue by visualising a tower with extremely muscular knees as he is bouncing the egg-headed Dennis on them, then visualise two beards (Sigmund Freud) cutting the muscular knee with a machete and finally visualise a giant muscular knee sitting on a psychiatrist couch as two white beards attempt to analyse the knee's problems.

The reader may notice that some images were combined to form a more complex image in a process called 'bundling'. This is similar to adding higher dimensions to the number lists and amounts to reducing the number of images necessary, but at the cost of added complexity. For example,")^2" was visualised as a tower with muscular knees- i.e. combining the leftmost symbol (the bracket) which is represented as a tower with the rightmost symbol (the power of 2) which is represented as a bodybuilding knee- the bodybuilding is due to the number 2 being set to the power. Performing such bundling avoided the need to create two separate pictures which could instead be easily combined into one image of a tower with muscular knees.

It is recommended to bundle items to reduce the images required, but not to the point of having such complex images that recall is hindered.

The reader should note that when a topic (say mathematics for this example) becomes familiar, some parts of the formula can be omitted, since knowledge of the subject provides you the information needed to complete the picture- thus the link serves as a tool to capture the data that is not familiar whilst your subject knowledge serves as the structure onto which this data is assembled. For example, in the equation above it was not necessary to memorise the brackets with the x between them if prior knowledge of the topic made it obvious that it is a function of x since- mu and sigma are the mean and variance and the only other variable left on the right hand side was x. Such shortcuts should always be used—remember that only what is unknown should be memorised.

Another important point to note is that once information is learnt, it should be used as a shortcut to memorise other information in which it appears. In mathematics, it means that once basic components have been memorised, committing to memory equations that contain them becomes very easy since images of the components already exist. For example, say we wanted to memorise the normal cumulative distribution function:

$$\Phi(x) = \frac{1}{\sigma\sqrt{2\pi}} \int\limits_{-\infty}^{x} e^{-\frac{(\mu-t)^2}{2\sigma^2}} \, dt$$

Combined with knowledge of the subject, all that is necessary to memorise the cumulative distribution function is to notice that it is simply the integral of the normal density function- so all we need to do is link camel (for cumulative) to interrogation light (for integral) and interrogation light to the wide bell (normal distribution).

From the above exposition, it is clear that a subject should be learnt from its basic principles towards its complex theories. This way, data learnt earlier can be used to more easily memorise the more complex ideas, as well as having a better structural knowledge onto which the information can be laid.

Chemistry notations

As with mathematical formulae, the approach used for chemistry notations employs the link system. The motivation should be to break down the structure into subcomponents whose images are established and can therefore be easily memorised. The procedure is as follows:

1. Ensure each symbol has a unique picture- write down a list to ensure no repetition.
2. Convert the name of the compound into an image.
3. Convert each component of the compound into an image- use names of sub-compounds if you are familiar with them (in the example below we do so for Amine).
4. Memorise from left to right.
5. Memorise from the top downwards.
6. For circular portions work clockwise.

The table below represents the unique identifiers we will be using for this example:

Symbol	Image	Why
Double bond	James bond with two heads	Double and Bond
Single bond	N/A	Assume it is a single bond if not otherwise specified
Letters	Corresponding image from the letter list	N/A
NH2	Preacher	Amine sounds like Amen

The reader should note that we have used the name of NH_2 to represents its image rather than memorise each element separately. This point was alluded to in the mathematical formulae and is again re-iterated here:

a. Previous knowledge of the topic should be used to make the conversion of data into images simpler- for example any group of items that are already known under a grouping name should be memorised as a group rather than the individual components (e.g. NH_2 is amine or in the mathematical example it was the normal density function that was known in the memorisation of the cumulative density function).

b. Structural knowledge of the topic should be used to avoid memorising data that can be reasoned- in the chemistry example below, we do not memorise single bonds thus assuming that unless an image of a double bond occurs we should assume a single bond is present. Further such reductions in data actually memorised are possible the more the practitioner is familiar with the general rules of the topic.

We proceed with the example of Melamine:

$$NH_2$$

Melamine sounds a bit like "melon mean"- which can be visualised as a mean looking melon. Continue by linking a mean looking melon to a preacher (Amine => Amen=> Preacher), perhaps this mean looking melon is preaching in front of a congregation, proceed by linking the preacher to a two headed James Bond- perhaps a gigantic two headed James Bond is sitting with the congregation nodding his head at the preacher's sermon, continue by linking a hen to the two headed James bond- perhaps the hen is the arch villain and is standing over the two headed James Bond boasting about the success of his evil scheme, proceed by linking a hen to a preacher- perhaps a hen is preaching to the other hens in the henhouse, again link the preacher to a double headed James Bond- perhaps this time the congregation consists of billions of such double headed James Bonds, proceed by linking James Bond to the hen- perhaps there is a double headed hen that is walking around an expensive dinner party with a tuxedo, then proceed to connecting a preacher and a hen-maybe a preacher outside on the farm is picking grains with his nose, proceed to linking the preacher to the double headed James bond-perhaps the double headed James Bond is walking around with preacher robes, finally proceed by linking the double headed James Bond to the Hen- perhaps the double headed James bond is picking grains with his noses.

The example above was deliberately used to illustrate a subtle point: the above approach works but there are plenty of repeated connections (e.g Hen connecting to Bond 3 times) that test the limits of the link system. In such situations there are two possible approaches:

a. Use the loci or peg system instead- repetitions in these systems cannot be confused.
b. Use 'bundling', as illustrated in the mathematical formulae section above- the aim is to bundle items in such a way to ensure that there are few repeated connections.

Method (b) is recommended; however, if the user would like to dedicate a large proportion of his loci system for his studies he may do so- the only disadvantage is that with formulae the loci system can get used up very quickly and new locations will have to be added (assuming a large amount of formulae and long term memory intentions).

With bundling, the above example is transformed to:

A preacher=> double headed hen with a tuxedo=>double headed preacher with a tuxedo=> hen preacher=> double headed hen with a tuxedo

An alternative bundling approach would be to bundle the circular portion into one image- for example we could think of a "hen ball"- a hen being used as a football (soccer ball) for example. If this approach is taken, any future circular structures should be treated similarly using a standard convention- the example above used the letter on the circumference to determine the type of ball it was. Note that doing this would require some basic knowledge of the topic to allow the types of bonds to be recalled.

This approach would lead to one simple picture to represent the entire structure- picture three preachers standing in a triangle

The name can be converted into: George = gorge and Bush= bush.

Proceed by pegging "gorge" to the "side swept grey hair" - perhaps you are walking near a gorge that is filled with gigantic side swept grey hair pieces instead of water. Then continue by linking "gorge" and "bush"- perhaps you walk near a row of bushes that have gorges on the stems instead of leaves.

Bernard Madoff- The admitted mastermind behind what has been described as the largest Ponzi scheme in history.

The distinctive feature to use is the large crooked nose or the thin lips.

The name can be converted into: Bernard = St. Bernard (dog breed that features in the movie Beethoven) and Madoff = "Mad off" which can be visualised as a mad off-button (typically a red button with a circle and a small vertical line) - so perhaps picture an off button with a straitjacket.

To combine the above, visualise a St. Bernard dog with the distinctive large crooked nose- blow it out of proportion, perhaps by making it so large and heavy that the dog is finding it difficult to get up. Continue by linking the off-button that is wearing a straitjacket with the dog- perhaps the dog is drooling billions of off-buttons that are wearing straitjackets and are running around like madmen.

The reader may note that it is simple to also add other facts to the link; for example we could add the fact that George Bush was the 43rd president by linking Bush to 43 (rim)- perhaps you are throwing gigantic bushes onto a basketball rim and none are getting through. The possibilities are limitless.

Presidents and Rulers

To memorise presidents, rulers or dynasties for that matter, we make use of one of the peg lists. It is up to the reader to decide which peg list is to be used for which task- in the examples below we will use the Effigy list.

We use the peg list assuming that the order of the information is important; in the case of presidents- it allows recall of the president by his ordinal position in the list of presidents.

The procedure is as follows:

1. Choose the peg list to use- ensure there are enough items on the list to memorise the entire block of new information.
2. Convert the name of the ruler/leader into an image.
3. Peg the image of the ruler/leader to the item from the list according to the position of the ruler/leader.
4. Link any other information required (such as date elected) to the leader's surname.

We will present an example with the first 3 presidents of the United States, leaving it to the reader to continue with the rest (note that the peg list chosen will have to be extended in order to memorise all presidents- alternatively you can use the number peg list which already has 101 items available within it):

1. George Washington, 1789
2. John Adams, 1797
3. Thomas Jefferson, 1801
4. James Madison, 1809
5. James Monroe, 1817

We proceed by using the effigy list:

For George Washington, remembering to stay consistent with our image for George (using "gorge" as we did with George Bush), we visualise a tree that instead of a trunk has a very long vertical gorge, then we link the gorge with a "washing town"- perhaps a gorge full of water is standing over a town carefully scrubbing the town centre.

To memorise the date we use the high dimensional approach (VWYZ) which results in the image of a brown duck that is exploding. Perhaps you see a brown duck being washed in the town centre whilst gradually it is becoming larger and finally explodes leaving the town gruesomely decorated.

Note that familiarity with the topic would allow the user to know the century and millennium in which a president was elected thus omitting the need to memorise the "17" portion of the date.

Continuing with the next president, John Adams; we use the image of an Adam's apple yawning to represent the name (Adam= Adam's apple, John= yawn). We peg this image to the second item on the effigy list, which is a swan- perhaps visualise a beautiful swan with a gigantic Adam's apple, all of a sudden the enormous Adam's apple is yawning with a thunderous noise- try to see and hear it clearly. To remember the date we proceed by linking pig to a yawning Adam's apple- perhaps you are in the middle of a pigsty but instead of pigs there are hundreds of yawning Adam's apples. Note that in this example we only used the last two digits of the date (97) instead of the entire year 1797- it is only necessary to memorise what you do not know, but since we already know that George Washington was elected in 1789 it is not necessary to memorise the "17" portion of the year. Such tricks and shortcuts are useful when memorising, they all boil down to the same concept—**only memorise what is completely new and unknown, then extrapolate using what you already know.**

The last example from the list would be to memorise the third president, Thomas Jefferson; to visualise the name, we could use the image of "Thomas the tank engine" to remember the first name and "chef fussing" to remember the surname. To peg the name to the effigy list, we use the image for number three, an ant, and we peg Thomas to it- visualise a large ant with a big smiley face pulling a train. To then link Thomas to Jefferson- perhaps visualise Thomas the tank engine with a chef's toque fussing over the soup- clearly see the concern and anxiety in his face. Finally to remember the year, 1801, we proceed by visualising suede (**suede** 0=s and 1= d, t) - perhaps the toque on the chef's head is made out of bright blue suede.

It is simple to extend this procedure to the other presidents:

James Madison, 1809 = Sail => Jam(s) Medicine=> Saab

James Monroe, 1817 = Hook=> Jam(s) Moon row=> Duck

...etc

This procedure can be applied to all other lists of rulers, dynasties and emperors.

Calendar

To plan the day, we frequently use a physical or digital calendar to assist in the process of memorising our appointments. Instead (or to complement), one could dedicate one of the previously created lists in order to store the day's appointments. The example below will use the Rhyme list- the procedure is as follows:

1. Assign a zero hour on your chosen list- do not change this mapping.

2. Peg each item on your agenda to the corresponding item on the chosen list.
3. For events that occur on half the hour, add a machete to the image which should indicate that the event starts at half the hour.
4. For events that last for longer than one hour simply peg the same item of the agenda to the two corresponding item on the list.

For example, say one wanted to remember tomorrow's schedule which consisted of:

Time	Appointment
08:00-09:00	Read the morning papers
09:00-10:00	Staff meeting
10:00-11:00	Inspect factory
11:00-12:00	Read the sales report
12:00-14:00	Lunch at *Chez Septime*
14:00-15:00	Interview candidates for a secretary role
15:00-16:00	Meet with the bank manager
16:00-17:00	Pick up the kids from school
17:00-18:00	Read the evening paper
18:00-19:00	Prepare dinner

Using the Rhyme list, we assign to each one of the 11 items on the list one hour of the working day (starting at 8am and ending at 7pm). To remember the first item on the agenda, we simply peg it to the first item on the rhyme list, Zorro- perhaps visualise a gigantic newspaper with a mask covering his eyes riding on the back of a horse rescuing a damsel in distress.

Next peg the second item on the agenda, staff meeting, to the second item on the rhyme list- a gun; perhaps you enter the staff meeting-room to see that around the table are sitting large shiny guns dressed up in suits ready for the meeting to begin instead of your company directors as you would have expected. Feel the shock and fear and smell the gun powder residue in the air.

Continue by pegging each item on the agenda to the corresponding item on rhyme list.

In order to recall the time of an event simply add the number on the rhyme list to your zero hour- which in the example above was 8am. For example, after memorising the list your partner calls to ask at what time you are having lunch that day- the number that comes to mind is 4, which you then add to 8 to remember that it is at 12. The zero hour was chosen to be 8am but in essence this could be any hour that suits the user, the key point is to then stay consistent and never change the zero hour after it was determined.

For those who wish to plan for more hours of the day, all that is necessary is to use one of the longer lists or simply to extend the rhyme list.

To plan for a month or a year ahead, it is advisable to use a different system. For example, planning for the month could easily be done using the grid system- each grid cell corresponds to one day of the month to whose image the agenda items are then pegged. So, peg the first item on that day's calendar to the grid cell's image and then link the rest of the calendar items in their order of occurrence.

Planning for the entire year could be done by using the phonetic alphabet to create an image for each hour of every date in the year; we could use a UVWXYZ approach where UVW is an image created using the phonetic alphabet and XYZ are the added dimensions. For example, say you had a doctor's appointment on the 12th of May at 10am- this could be represented numerically as 120510 (using a dd/mm/hh date convention)- we then create an image for 120, which is phonetically represented by t,d/n/s,z- a possible image could be "Tennis", perhaps visualise a tennis ball.

The next three numbers 510 each represent a dimension as illustrated earlier in this section- in this case we would visualise a "Red tennis ball parachuting in outer space"- all that remains is to link this image to the appointment item which is doctor- perhaps visualise this red tennis ball parachuting in outer space injuring itself by landing on a pointy corner of a star and then rushing quickly to see the doctor for help.

Similarly, birthdays can be remembered in the same way but using the convention VWYZ instead to represent the day and month (as dd/mm) - VW is the number taken from the phonetic alphabet list whilst YZ are the two added dimensions.

A powerful combination of techniques would be to remember a person's name and then link the birthday to the image of the name. The sequence would be as follows:

Distinctive feature image=>First name image=> Surname image=>birthday image

Please note that as always, if bundling is possible the steps above can be reduced to, for example:

Distinctive feature image=> Name and Surname image => birthday image

Oenophiles

To remember the characteristics of a particular collection of fine wines, we would use the loci system. In particular it is recommended to use a palace, a large house or a museum as the location. The procedure is as follows:

1. Assign each wine a room in the palace.
2. Peg the name of the wine to the entrance.

3. Peg the year of the wine to the first item in the room.
4. Peg the properties of the wine to the rest of the items in the room.
5. Work clockwise around the palace from the bottom up.
6. Work clockwise around each room.

For illustration purposes we will use a palace that has the following rooms and items at the start (the reader is advised to use a location that is familiar to him as discussed in the section describing the loci method):

1. Entrance Hall- Chandelier, Fountain, Vase, portrait, Gold statue and stairs.
2. Dining room- Serving table, Knight's armour, Long dining table and balcony.
3. Kitchen- coat hangers, sink, stove, preparation table, pots and pans hanging, microwave and fridge.

The list of wines and their descriptions to be memorised are as follows:

Dom. Romane Conti 1997 -

A French dark red Burgundy wine that smells of berries, spices and leather. It hints at flavours of soy sauce, flowers and liquorice.

Petrus Pomerol 1998-

A purple Merlot. Extremely fruity- suggestions of berries, vanilla, mocha, and oak

Barbaresco Cayun Martinenga 1986

It smells of rose, leather, mushroom, toffee and rhubarb tart

We begin the journey in the entrance hall, pegging a gigantic millennium dome counting roman soldiers as they march through the entrance to the palace (to remember the name of the wine is Dom. Romane Conti). We proceed to the first item in the entrance hall (chandelier) and peg to it the year of the wine (1997) - perhaps visualise that the chandelier is made of lots of pigs holding candles instead of the usual shiny crystals that a chandelier usually has.

Proceed to the next items in the room and peg to each the properties of the wine; in this case we would visualise a fountain that is gushing lots of dark red liquid that is holding the French flag. We then visualise a vase that is smelling a jar of spices and begins to sneeze loudly shaking the entire room with every sneeze. We then look at the portrait and see berries in tight leather clothing posing. Then we walk past the golden statue and as we do so he stops to offer us a bunch of flowers that have soy sauce bottles instead of petals. Finally as we walk up the stairs we see a gigantic liquorice (picture the round black candy roll) running down the stairs leaving sticky footmarks on the beautiful red carpet.

Continuing the journey by entering the dining room, to remember the 2nd wine's name we convert it into an image which can be visualised- perhaps a Pet wrestling with a bull that has poles instead of legs (Petrus= Pet Wrestle, Pomerol=Pole Meryl- Meryl was visualised by thinking of the bull in the Merrill Lynch logo)- peg this image to the dining room entrance- perhaps the pet and the bull with the pole legs are ferociously wrestling near the door smashing against it with every tug and push until it breaks (see the image, hear the sounds and feel the violent atmosphere). Proceed by pegging the year (98) to the serving table- perhaps a waiter has put a gigantic bath (for 98) on top of the serving table from which he is dishing out the food. Next, peg the properties of the wine to the rest of the items in the room- visualise the armour melting into a gooey purple substance to remember that it is a purple merlot. Then visualise berries sitting around the dining table each with a huge cone of vanilla ice-cream- to remember the first two suggested flavours. Finally visualise an oak tree that is mocha coloured standing on the balcony peering to the distance.

Proceed with the next wine and any others you may wish to add to the list, the sequence for the third wine would be:

Barbaresco Cayun Martinenga pegged to the Kitchen entrance => 86 pegged to the coat hangers => smells pegged to the rest of the items in the Kitchen

It is recommended to use a location you are familiar with, but after following the location provided above by the author and after running through the images created, the practitioner may begin to sense some familiarity to the location created. This is an excellent illustration of how to build an imaginary palace of memories- for those that wish to experiment with this, simply create a new room as you try to remember another classic wine.

After the palace is built, reviewing the material can be almost as pleasurable as experiencing the wine in real life. With practise of the techniques introduced in the concentration section of this manual, going through each room in the palace will elicit the smells and tastes of the wine that the room represents. The learning experience is now no longer a boring rote procedure but actually a thing to look forward to in every day.

Other applications and extensions

We provide other learning tasks that are similar to those already covered and include the appropriate system to use:

Chess openings- Use the loci system; assign a palace (or a town) to represent all chess openings, then each room in the palace (or house in the town) would contain the details of one opening- the name is pegged to the entrance and the moves are pegged to the items in that room of the palace (or house in the case of town).

The standard chess notation can be broken down into unique identifiers which can then be used as images of the moves involved in the opening. One simple suggestion is to convert each move into a number- e.g. e4 c5 can be converted into 5435 which can be represented by an image using the high dimensional convention VWYZ. Other notations of a move as well as the pieces involved (which are better visualised as their 3D physical object rather than the notation letter which represents them) can be bundled into the image.

Corporate hierarchy- Use the grid method with the CEO/President on the top row working downward. A useful modification may be to use a triangular grid.

Equity Volsurface- use the grid approach, which can be adapted by using the option strikes as the first row, option maturities as the first column and the option volatility as the entry in each cell to be memorised. Peg each image for the volatility (convert the number into an image) to the image of that cell on the grid.

Maps- Use either the rectangular grid or the circular grid approach depending on the structural form of the city or country being memorised. At each grid point memorise a key road of place name that is dominant in that cell.

Then use the link system, starting with a major highway, linking any roads that lead off this highway; then repeat for other major roads and finally side streets. Work from major to minor and work grid point by grid point on your map ensuring systematic coverage of the data- i.e. work your way from left to right and from bottom to top (west to east and south to north). When memorising the roads as they lead off a highway, indicate whether it is a left turn or a right turn by adding identifiers for left and right (perhaps a wristwatch for left and a boxing glove for right) and bundle them into the picture.

Morse code- Use the phonetic system- represent a dash with the letters "t,d" and represent dot with the letter "r"; then create a word for each letter in the alphabet by finding a word that is formed by the dots and dashes which represent it in Morse code. For example "A" in Morse code is ". _" which using the system above can be either "rt" or "rd", so we could use "rat", "rot" or "rod" to represent the letter A- choose one. Proceed by creating a unique image for each letter.

Paintings- use the link system:

Pick a distinctive feature of the painting or use the painting itself as the setting for your image=> link the name of the painting=> link the artist's name

Perfumes- use the loci room system in the same manner as applied to wines

Philatelists- use the link system:

Pick a distinctive feature of the stamp or the stamp image itself=> link the name of the stamp=> link the year

Poems- use the link system as follows:

Name of the poem=> linked to the first word (or bundle of words)=> proceed by linking each word in the poem to the next bundle thus connecting words such as "of", "and", "then", "than"...etc, into one image.

Note that in most cases it is better and faster to ignore connecting words and to just memorise the key words of each line- after reviewing a few times, the connecting words will usually be captured accurately.

Recipes – use the link system as follows:

Name of recipe=> linked to the first step in the procedure =>linked to the following steps with bundling of quantities or temperatures into the images

Alternatively, one can use the loci room system assigning a room to each recipe and thus create a palace of recipes.

Tube/Underground map- use either the grid system for the entire map or use the link system to link the stations on each train route.

Building your own system

After following the examples presented above, the reader can identify the pattern and build his own system to suit his needs, keeping in mind the following key points:

1. Break down the data into the unique components that make up the topic.
2. Provide an image for each component- ensure there are no conflicts (both internally and with other topics you have already covered).
3. Choose the system that is most appropriate (e.g. loci for sequences and link for connecting 2 items).
4. Apply consistently and do not change nor make exceptions.

Most important and to re-iterate an earlier point- for long term retention you must REVIEW, REVIEW, and REVIEW- as per the recommended review schedule. Otherwise the information is only available for a short period of time.

Training plan

In order to master the techniques presented in this chapter, the reader is recommended to follow the schedule presented below. The key point to note is that the optimal approach to mastering a skill is through its incorporation into daily activities.

Week 1-4 – Becoming familiar with the systems

1. Commit to memory at the very least the following information:
   a. Phonetic alphabet list from 0-100: this can be done by memorising 10 words every day and revising the words already learnt from the previous days at the start of every session.
   b. Alphabet list
   c. Effigy list
   d. Rhyme list
   e. Body list
   f. Basic Grids
   g. Create at least 3 loci: 1 with at least 100 monuments/items and 2 with at least 20 monuments/items.
2. Learn 5 new words every day: this can be words encountered in reading, conversation, TV etc which you are not familiar with- simply note them down, look up their meaning and memorise using the system- make sure you review as instructed for long term retention. If you cannot find 5 new words a day, simply search the internet or dictionary (word-a-day websites are quite good).
3. Memorise the name of any new person you encounter- be it on TV, internet or real life.
4. Memorise any numbers you encounter through the day- it could be a stock index, price, or a phone number- get into the

habit of breaking these down into images and memorising them. (Note that review is not necessary for items you do not wish to store in long term memory).

Week 4-8- Incorporate into daily life

Continue with the habits formed above but also add/modify:

1. Learn 10 new words every day.
2. Memorise your shopping list and try to do your shopping without looking down at the written version.
3. Try dialling phone numbers you have memorised without using the phonebook (be it digital or physical).
4. Memorise your day's calendar and try to think about your day without referring to the written down version.
5. Go for a drive, bicycle ride or walk to new places- this will increase the loci available to you. Then mentally review the journey several times and map out the monuments to use. It is advisable to be systematic in the coverage of the territory in order to gradually build gigantic loci.

Week 8- onwards

Continue with the habits formed above but also add:

1. Begin learning a new language- using the techniques above to memorise new words.
2. Commit to memory any new fact or figure you come across.
3. Read about 3 new topics in the encyclopaedia every day and memorise the key facts
4. If you are interested in memory championships, start charting your progress, the list below includes simple methods to achieve this:
   a. Time how long it takes you to memorise a pack of cards.
   b. Time how long it takes you to recall the pack of cards and how many errors you made.

c. How many cards you can memorise in 10 minutes.

d. How many binary digits you can memorise in 1 minute.

e. To chart progress, it is important that the test be consistent; for example memorising words may be more worthy since you are actually learning something useful, but some words can be easier to remember compared to others thus making accurate progress charting impossible. To avoid wasting time on *de minimis* simply limit the amount of time spent on testing- do it only to chart progress- 10 minutes twice a week may be sufficient as a start. The rest of the time, practise your memory skills with things that matter- this way you kill two birds with one stone.

5. Extend the lists to provide you with more pegs and allow for more possibilities

6. Extend your loci and add new loci all the time.

7. Ensure you are spending an adequate amount of time on reviewing- this is crucial for long term memory.

8. Explore other areas to which the systems can be applied, adapt the systems for your purposes if need be.

Summary and Revision-map

Key points

- The gluing mechanism used in memory techniques involves vivid exaggerated imagery, ludicrous nonsensical action, lots of colours as well the involvement of as many senses and emotions as possible in such a scene.
- The link system involves "gluing" each new item to the next- forming a chain of images each connected to the previous and the next.
- The peg system involves "gluing" each new item to an item that is already known from previously established lists.
- The loci system involves "gluing" new information to items that are already known and are in fact part of a physical location familiar to the user.
- The grid approach is used to memorise visual data by "gluing" the details onto the image of the item that represents the cell.
- The purpose of the ready-made lists and loci is to have a large amount of possible pegs as well as an efficient way of filing data.
- Data should always be broken down into key components and unique identifiers which are then used in the application of the systems.
- Dimensions and bundling can be used to incorporate more data into each image as well as reduce the repetitions of single pieces of information.
- Review should be done within the optimal windows and is absolutely essential for long term storage.

Revision-Map

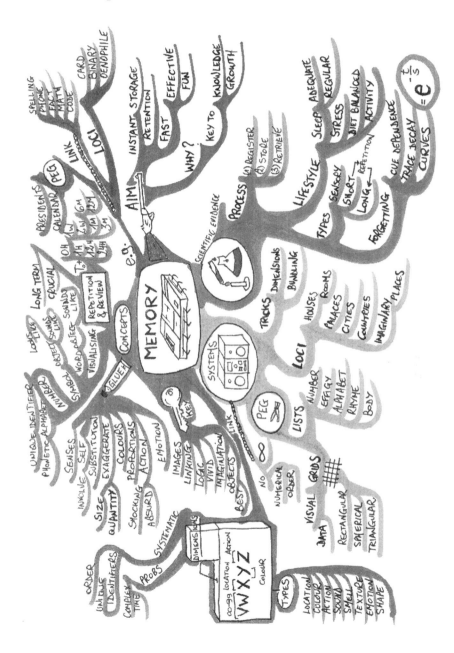

Part 3- Speed Reading

I took a speed reading course and read 'War and Peace' in twenty minutes. It involves Russia.

Woody Allen

Aims

- Read faster,
- And maintain or increase comprehension.

Introduction

There is a great deal of controversy about speed reading; it derives from some unverified claims by purveyors of courses on the topic, and from more pseudo-scientific treatment of the next evolution of speed reading. The latter is a subconscious photographic-type reading, which claims reading rates that are even more difficult to believe. Woody Allen's famous joke on the topic sums up the argument.

There are many courses available on the topic and these are generally split into two genres:

1. Traditional speed reading.
2. Subconscious Photographic-type reading.

The traditional type of speed reading focuses on improving the mechanics of reading- the main focus is on minimising regressions during reading, usually through the use of a guide, reducing sub-vocalisation and capturing more words with each glance. The approach involves performing drills daily in order to maintain the skill.

The second approach, which involves using the subconscious mind in order to capture the information, is a more recent development (though some courses date back to the 1970s) and it offers a very different approach to reading when compared to the traditional speed reading courses. The key idea is to enter deeper levels of the mind, at which the subconscious mind is able capture the information desired at rates that are faster than what is possible with the conscious mind alone.

Both genres have a wide range of advertised reading speeds that are attainable using the system. Traditional speed reading courses claim that practitioners can achieve reading speeds of up to 5000wpm

(wpm=Words per minute), whilst subconscious photographic reading systems often claim speeds of over 25000wpm, together with high comprehension, are easily attainable.

The author's experience suggests that there is some merit to both systems but that advertised reading rates are not as pervasive among practitioners as is commonly advertised. Additionally, it is difficult to comprehend how 25000wpm is attainable by most people if the 6-time world record holder Anne Jones can only read at around 4200wpm. Such inconsistencies are most likely driven by overzealous marketing, which can be attributed to operating in a fiercely competitive industry; and thus, it should not put one off from using the techniques.

There are clear advantages of using both types of speed reading methods and the aim of this chapter is to provide a simple system that combines the best of both approaches with strong emphasis on traditional training routines. The aim is to have a powerful pragmatic reading technique that increases both speed and comprehension. To make fantastical claims on the reading speeds possible with the technique below would cause unnecessary anxiety and anticipation for the practitioner- the simple aim of reading faster and understanding more should be the only goal, and anything else that is attained on top of that is a bonus.

The key to the technique is regular practise- the best analogy is that of competitive sports or bodybuilding: any gains made through hard work and diligent training is lost if this level of training is not maintained. However, the main difference is that, with reading drills, one is able to choose the topic on which to practise and can in essence spend drill time on reading what would have needed to be read anyway- thus making training-time costless.

Lastly, it is important to recognise that different reading materials require different reading speeds. This is a point that is largely ignored in the propaganda of reading rates- to be able to read at 1000wpm does not mean that such speeds are applicable to reading an advanced mathematics textbook to which the reader has had little previous exposure. Some topics require logical reasoning that cannot be performed by simply reading the material (mathematical proofs that use novel concepts to arrive at the proof's conclusion is a quintessential example) - it is therefore unrealistic to expect high reading speeds through such topics. Thus, to judge and measure your reading speed, it is necessary to always compare across a similar type of material- a modern novel appears as the best candidate and will be the tool used below.

Scientific Evidence

Reading is considered a complex cognitive process during which symbols are decoded to extract the meaning that the author attempted to portray. A certain mastery of the cognitive processes is required in order for the decoding procedure to become automatic, so that the attention can be focused on understanding the concepts being discussed.

The physical process of reading involves a series of eye fixations which can focus either on individual words or groups of words. Research has shown that fast readers tend to have less fixations but that each fixation encompasses a larger proportion of the text.

A very early discovery made by the US Air force showed that with training, flashing 4 words on a screen at a rate of 2 milliseconds between each group of 4 words was fully recognised by the practitioner. The term for the technique was called Rapid Serial Visual Presentation and in the 1940s it formed the main approach to improving reading speeds.

Early research that followed suggested that speed reading was only a skimming tool allowing the reader to glean key points from the material being read, though later studies indicated that even as reading speed increased comprehension also improved (see Cranney, Brown, Hansen, and Inouye 1982).

More recent research into the latest brand of speed reading, the subconscious type of reading (e.g. Photoreading), suggests that the reading speeds attained by practitioners are far lower than the claims marketed and appear to actually be close to normal reading speeds (see McNamara D.S. "Preliminary analysis of photoreading" which was prepared for NASA).

Technique

It is important to view speed reading as just a technique- focusing very little attention on the method and more attention on the reading. It is common for practitioners to get obsessed about their progress and whether their technique is correct, which often causes poor performance.

The concepts are simple; the reader is advised not to try and extract hidden ideas or deeper meaning (since there are none) but to just follow the procedure as instructed, focusing mainly on the reading. The crux of the method is by performing the drills daily without fail- measurable progress will then indicate whether the technique is having an effect.

The key ingredients to the system are as follows:

1. Concentration on the reading and blocking out distractions.
2. Avoiding regressions.
3. Reducing sub-vocalisation.
4. Capturing more words with each fixation.
5. Using layered reading.
6. Using subconscious reading for increased familiarity with a topic.

It is important to develop the habit to include all the above concepts whenever you are reading- irrespective of the subject matter.

Concentration

This topic was covered in depth in the first chapter since it is a crucial ingredient for any learning experience. Since reading is perhaps the ultimate learning tool, concentration is thus a key ingredient. Having the mind wander when one is reading causes frustration (due to having to repeatedly read the same sentence or page) and makes the whole process less efficient as well as far less pleasurable.

Practising the concentration techniques introduced earlier are crucial for the implementation of the reading technique presented below. **Every reading session should start with a brief 5 minutes concentration exercise that acts as a centring mechanism for the learning experience which will follow.**

Regressions

Regression is the term used to describe when a reader has to stop the flow of reading and repeat a sentence or a paragraph that has just been read- this is usually due to either a lapse in concentration or the complexity of the topic.

In order to avoid regressions, there are two key tools: the first is to improve concentration whilst the second is to use a "guide". Since the concentration was already covered in great detail, this section will focus on the second tool- the "guide".

Using a "guide" refers to employing an aid that would lead the reader through the passage without having to stop or repeat any of the material. The aid is there to provide rhythm and pace the reading according to the practitioner's skill. Most traditional reading techniques put great emphasis on using the hands as a guide and generally introduce several hand motions that the user should use through different reading material. The author's experience suggests that focusing on different hand motions again puts too much focus on the technique and less focus on the reading. Therefore, the system below uses only 2 simple hand motions, one for skimming and the other for reading.

The keys to using the hand as a "guide" are as follows:

1. Keep the hand moving in a rhythmic pace that is manageable given your current reading abilities- skimming should be fast and the aim should be to get the general content of the topic being read, whilst the main reading motion should be slower and focus on higher comprehension.

2. Follow the hand, never fall behind it and never go back (regress) - if something has been missed it can be pencilled on the margin with a question mark and can be re-read once the full read through the material has been completed. This is a much better way to learn- the simple concepts and the basics get captured in the first read through, whilst more complex details and subtleties get added on subsequent reading, and thus building a much better structural understanding of the topic.

3. Do not focus on the hand nor pay too much attention to the motion- the key is to move rhythmically through the text focusing only on the reading and avoiding regressions.

Hand motions

1. Skimming: use an S-shaped motion through the page
    a. Perform an S-type motion with the hand flat on the page and the tip of the middle finger drawing the shape as presented below.
    b. Start and end each motion about one third away from either side of the text.
    c. Keep up with the hand, do not regress; if you miss something it is not important, you will get to it in the next phase of the reading process.
    d. Do not focus much on the hand movement- all the attention should be on the reading; the hand is only used to guide you rhythmically and to ensure no regression is taking place.
    e. This hand motion is for fast reading- mainly used in skimming through the material.
    f. The diagram below illustrates the hand motion.

XXXXXXXXXXXXXXXXXXXXXXXXXXXXXXXXXXXX
XXXXXXXXXXXXXXXXXXXXXXXXXXXXXXXXXXXX
XXXXXXXXXXXXXXXXXXXXXXXXXXXXXXXXXXXX
XXXXXXXXXXXXXXXXXXXXXXXXXXXXXXXXXXXX
XXXXXXXXXXXXXXXXXXXXXXXXXXXXXXXXXXXX
XXXXXXXXXXXXXXXXXXXXXXXXXXXXXXXXXXXX
XXXXXXXXXXXXXXXXXXXXXXXXXXXXXXXXXXXX
XXXXXXXXXXXXXXXXXXXXXXXXXXXXXXXXXXXX
XXXXXXXXXXXXXXXXXXXXXXXXXXXXXXXXXXXX
XXXXXXXXXXXXXXXXXXXXXXXXXXXXXXXXXXXX
XXXXXXXXXXXXXXXXXXXXXXXXXXXXXXXXXXXX
XXXXXXXXXXXXXXXXXXXXXXXXXXXXXXXXXXXX
XXXXXXXXXXXXXXXXXXXXXXXXXXXXXXXXXXXX
XXXXXXXXXXXXXXXXXXXXXXXXXXXXXXXXXXXX
XXXXXXXXXXXXXXXXXXXXXXXXXXXXXXXXXXXX
XXXXXXXXXXXXXXXXXXXXXXXXXXXXXXXXXXXX
XXXXXXXXXXXXXXXXXXXXXXXXXXXXXXXXXXXX
XXXXXXXXXXXXXXXXXXXXXXXXXXXXXXXXXXXX

2. Reading: vertical line
   a. The hand motion used for reading is simply a vertical line that runs down the middle of the text.
   b. Perform the motion with the hand flat on the page and the tip of the middle finger drawing the shape presented below.
   c. Keep up with the hand, do not regress; if you miss something it is not important, you will get to it in the next phase of the reading process.
   d. Do not focus much on the hand movement- all the attention should be on the reading; the hand is only used

to guide you rhythmically and to ensure no regression is taking place.

e. This hand motion is used for all reading purposes except skimming.

a. The diagram below illustrates the hand motion.

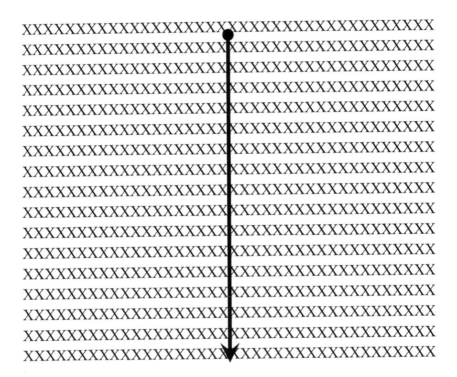

The key point about regressions is to keep going through the material without stopping for anything; it is important to annotate portions that have not been understood for further focus in later reading, but aim to keep the pace of reading undisturbed- come back to any difficult points (as annotated) after finishing a full read through the material. This requires discipline and confidence in the technique- both should develop with practise.

The idea of no-stopping obviously extends to flipping pages- make it quick and efficient- have the hand that is not being used as a guide ready to flip the page as you near its bottom.

Sub-vocalisation

Sub-vocalisation is the process of reading word by word, pronouncing them mentally and sometimes even moving the lips with the pronunciation. Such an approach to reading essentially takes a visual input, converts it into an audio output which then gets converted into a concept.

It is generally accepted that reading at higher speeds requires removing the need to translate words into sounds and simply transforming visual inputs straight into the concept that they represent.

There is some disagreement among practitioners about whether sub-vocalisation should be eliminated completely, but there is clear agreement that it should be minimised.

The system below relies on performing the drills regularly in order to reduce sub-vocalisation; the approach focuses on developing habits that would minimise the need to transform words into their audio interpretation.

The key involves saying one word for each fixation- so using the skimming technique for example- each fixation would capture 3 half lines but would only involve mentally pronouncing one of the words in those 3 half lines. The same applies to the vertical line technique- each fixation captures half a line but only one word gets pronounced.

Being able to transform a block of words straight into their concept without the need to verbalise the individual components is key to breaking into high speeds of reading. The "sound" barrier is usually estimated to be at about 600wpm- reading faster than this is not possible while sub-vocalising (noting that the world's fastest speaker, Steve Woodmore, can speak at a rate of 637wpm whilst the previous Guinness book of world record's holder, John Moschitta. Jr, could speak at 586wpm).

Fixations

When we read, we do not flow through the material smoothly but instead we perform many mini-fixations which for most readers involve gazing at 1-2 words at a time, getting their meaning, and then moving to the next 1-2 words and so on through the text. Reading is essentially a series of jumps between groups of words.

The inefficient reader generally gazes at every word, this therefore increases the number of pauses required to run through the same material. The goal is therefore to increase the amount of words that are read at every such pause; this would mean that one would be able to go through the material with far less pauses, thus increasing speed. The other benefit is that the stringing of individual words into a concept is replaced with capturing an entire concept with each glance- this has advantages in terms of comprehension, since less focus is required on tracking and connecting the data, with more attention left to focus on the concept itself.

The approach to increase the content in each fixation involves training drills that increase peripheral vision, and comprehension drills that allow one to understand the concept represented by a bunch of words instead of having to read each word at a time and then build the concept along the way.

The use of the hand motion organises the sequence of fixations through the text; the circles in the diagrams below illustrate where to focus the attention as the hand moves down the text. It is crucial to note that:

   a. Fixations should take about 1-2 seconds each and the eyes should not be moving during the fixation period- the eyes should focus only on the point of fixation (illustrated as an inner circle in the diagrams below).

   b. The eyes should focus on the point of fixation but should capture everything else in the region of fixation using peripheral vision (regions of fixation are the ellipses illustrated below).

   c. Practise is required to increase the size of the fixation region- the drills at the end of the chapter are necessary to achieve this purpose.

For the skimming hand motion, the circle illustrates the point of fixation, the ellipse illustrates the region of fixation, whilst the number boxes illustrate the sequence- i.e. the first fixation region is the ellipse below box one, the second fixation is below box 2, the third is next to box three...etc. Note that the skimming method requires fixation of 3 half lines: the eyes should focus in the middle of the fixation region, peripherally seeing the entire region- this point of focus is illustrated by the inner circle in the fourth fixation region. Also note (for skimming) that the sequence of fixation is not the standard left to right but instead it is left right then right left then left right again. This approach works well for skimming and allows the capturing of the general content.

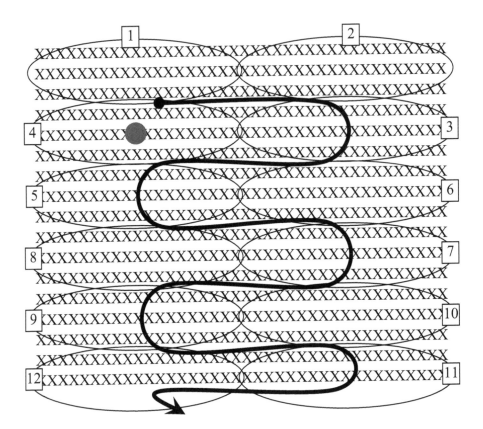

For the main reading hand motion, using a vertical line, the fixation is done left to right as with normal reading approaches. Each fixation contains one half of a line- the eyes should focus in the middle of the half-line and see the rest of the words peripherally. This point is illustrated by the inner circle in the third fixation as an example:

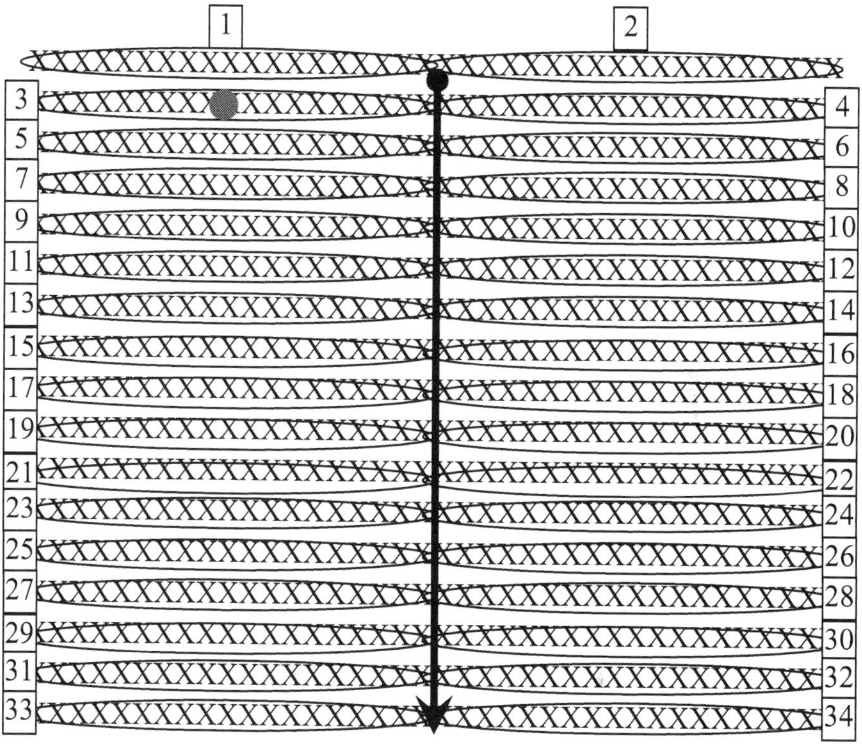
1
2
3
4
5
6
7
8
9
10
11
12
13
14
15
16
17
18
19
20
21
22
23
24
25
26
27
28
29
30
31
32
33
34

Layered reading

Layered reading is the process of breaking reading into several layers, and with each layer the coverage of the topic becomes deeper.

The advantage of layered reading is that any information that does not get captured in early layers gets learnt in later layers. This is an advantage because it allows the reader to **flow** through the material in a relaxed manner, knowing that anything missed can be added later- it thus promotes the minimisation of any tendency to regress. The second advantage is that such layering of the learning experience results in a more efficient uptake of the information- learning the simple aspects and basics first provides a firm structure onto which more complicated information can be constructed and understood in a much more coherent manner.

Layered reading is recommended for any long reading sessions that are non-leisure type reading- the main candidates for **not** using layered reading would be reading novels or reading headlines.

The key steps in the layered reading are as follows:

1. Previewing- this process should take at most 5 minutes and involves reading the back cover, the table of contents and having a quick glance at the structure of the book.
2. Skimming- this process involves reading through the entire book using the skimming hand motion- the focus should be on extracting the general themes of the book.
3. Speed reading- this process involves reading through the entire book using the vertical hand motion- the aim should be on understanding the deeper details of all the topics in the book (noting down question marks along the way for parts that need revisiting).
4. Review- this process involves going through the material once more using the skimming hand motion but slowing

down at sections with question marks- reading through these much slower- the aim is to review everything that has been read and to complete the gaps on anything that has not been understood.

If properly performed, the time spent should be less than with the standard reading approach and the comprehension should be higher.

Get into the habit of following the layered reading approach with everything in your daily life; typical examples would be memos, long e-mails, technical reading, textbooks, academic papers etc...

Subconscious reading (optional)

The author's experience with the subconscious reading system suggests that, even though the high reading rates claimed are not attainable by all, the ability to understand the topic seems much higher when performing an initial subconscious read through the material. It is for this reason that this technique has been included- although optional, it is a recommended addition for the layered reading of any topic being studied.

The procedure is as follows:

1. Sit with the book on the table in front of you.
2. Close your eyes.
3. Spend 5 minutes using your favourite concentration technique to enter a deeper state of mind- Buddhist breathing is recommended.
4. Mentally state the name of the book and your purpose for reading it.
5. Focus your attention on the top back of your head for a few moments until you feel your eyes relax and your peripheral vision expand (spend 1-2 minutes).

6. Open your eyes but do not focus them.
7. Open the book on the first page with content on it- ensure that your field of vision covers the entire two pages- you should be able to see the four corners of the book. The main point to note is that the eyes should not be focused- you should **not** be able to read the words on the page- you only need to be able to capture the content of the two pages in your glance- **do not try to read!** The aim is for your subconscious mind to capture (photograph) the information. It will all seem blurry but that is the goal, just capture the entire 2 pages at one glance and do not focus on any word, phrase or picture- again do not try and read.
8. Flip through the pages at a rhythmic pace- with every turn of the page ensure you maintain your defocused gaze. (Aim for 1 second per flip).
9. Ensure you maintain your relaxed state as you flip through the pages; if your mind begins to wander, simply let go (as with the concentration exercises) and continue flipping through the pages. The whole experience should feel more like a relaxation exercise rather than reading.
10. Once finished, affirm to yourself that your mind has absorbed all the information in the book and it will be made available when reading through it.
11. Close your eyes and spend another 5 minutes with your favourite concentration technique.
12. Take a break of at least 1 hour to allow for the processing of the information.

This subconscious reading procedure should be done before skimming- the main goal is to get the subconscious mind familiar with the topic, with the aim that the information will then be made conscious during the other layered reading parts.

As stated in the introduction, this process alone does not produce high reading rates; we use it here as an addition to the layered reading approach, with the main goal of extracting a better structural foundation of the topic- which should make the whole reading process easier and produce better comprehension. This is an optional step in the reading system.

Therefore, the overall layered reading procedure becomes as follows:

1. Previewing- this process should take at most 5 minutes and involves reading the back cover, the table of contents and having a quick glance at the structure of the book.
2. Subconscious reading (optional) – this process allows your subconscious mind to capture the information in the book and build a structural understanding of the topic, as well as promote comprehension and easier reading through the material.
3. Skimming- this process involves reading through the entire book using the skimming hand motion- the focus should be on extracting the general themes of the book.
4. Speed reading- this process involves reading through the entire book using the vertical hand motion- the aim should be on understanding the deeper details of all the topics in the book (noting down question marks along the way for parts that need revisiting).
5. Review- this process involves going through the material once more using the skimming hand motion but slowing down at sections with question marks, reading through these much slower- the aim is to review everything that has been read and to complete the gaps on anything that has not been understood during the previous passage through the material.

(For the interested reader, the best exposition of subconscious type reading, at least in this author's opinion, is Paul Scheele's

PhotoReading book- this resource is extremely well presented and has some very thought-provoking ideas)

Varying reading speeds

It is important to note that reading speeds should and would differ according to the complexity of the subject being read. It is therefore important to pace the hand motion at the speed which is most appropriate for the subject being read- the key is to go as fast as possible without compromising comprehension.

Irrespective of the speed that has been chosen, the key is to always stick to the speed reading principles of: concentration, avoiding regressions, reducing sub-vocalisation, capturing more words with each fixation and using layered reading- at the beginning, some of these will not come naturally, but with time and training it will eventually be the only way you would feel comfortable reading.

Training plan

The crux to speed reading is the regular routine of drills; without training on a daily basis, it is not possible to maintain high speeds nor is it possible to develop them in the first place.

For the reading drills, it is recommended to use simple reading material (a novel is a good example) rather than complicated technical material with which reading speeds can vary depending on your familiarity with the topic.

Again, to kill two birds with one stone, the practitioner may choose to train with material that is on his compulsory reading list but the above consideration regarding technical reading should be kept in mind. However, for the measurement of progress, the practitioner is recommended to use a modern novel since its complexity is likely to stay consistent whilst other reading materials are likely to vary depending on the topic- thus making the ability to accurately chart progress more difficult.

To calculate reading speeds, simply approximate the number of words on a page by counting the number of words in a typical row and multiply by the number of rows. Then calculate the number of pages read divided by the time taken (in minutes) - this would provide your Words Per Minute reading speed (WPM). It is recommended to chart progress once a week.

In all the exercises, it is important to remove any worries or anxiety about comprehension; at times, you will be reading at higher speeds or fixating on more words than you are capable of understanding at present- the key is to let go and follow the exercise instructions and try to reach the targets set. The practitioner must stay concentrated on the training and keep his attention on the reading, even if it is too fast to fully comprehend. The whole point of the training/drills is to feel free to push against the current boundaries in order to improve the speed at which you read with high comprehension and comfort.

(Note it is advisable to use a stopwatch for the following exercises in order to measure the time as instructed- a countdown alarm function is best in order to avoid the need to check the time left).

Exercise 1- Speed and comprehension

1. Take the reading material chosen for the practise and begin reading at a comfortable reading rate for 5 minutes using the vertical hand motion- the aim should be to read with full comprehension. (note the page on which you started).
2. Note the point in the book to which you arrived after 5 minutes.
3. Read through the material again (using the same hand motion) but increase your speed and aim to arrive at the same ending point (noted in point 2 above) in 4 minutes instead of five.
4. Repeat again but this time aim to complete in 3 minutes.
5. Repeat again but this time aim to complete in 2 minutes.
6. Repeat again, **this time using the skimming hand motion,** and aim to complete the same material in 1 minute.
7. Finally, starting at the end point noted in step 2 above, read with your comfortable reading rate for 1 minute.
8. Once a week note down the reading speed attained in step 7 above by noting the number of words read in that 1 minute. (number of pages read multiplied by the number of words per page).

Exercise 2- Speed

1. Take the reading material chosen for the practise and begin reading at a comfortable reading rate for 3 minutes using the vertical hand motion- the aim should be to read with full comprehension. (Note the page on which you started).

2. Note the point in the book to which you arrived after 3 minutes.

3. Count the number of pages read, and add this to the end point noted in step 2 above- this is your new target end point.

4. Read through the material again (using the same hand motion) but increase your speed and aim to arrive at the new ending point (noted in step 3 above) in 3 minutes.

5. Increase the end point again by adding the same amount (the amount read in step 1) to the new end point from point 3 above- this is the new end point. For example if you read 3 pages in 3 minutes, the end point for step 4 would be 6 pages whilst the end point for step 5 would be 9 pages.

6. Read through the material again (using the same hand motion) but increase your speed and aim to arrive at the new ending point (noted in step 5 above) in 3 minutes.

7. Increase the amount of pages one last time- so in the example above you now need to read 12 pages.

8. Read through the material again, **this time using the skimming hand motion**, but increase your speed and aim to arrive at the new ending point (noted in step 7 above) in 3 minutes.

9. Finally, starting at the end point noted in step 2 above, read with your comfortable reading rate for 1 minute.

10. Once a week note down the reading speed attained in step 9 above by noting the number of words read in that 1 minute. (number of page read multiplied by the number of words per page).

Exercise 3- Peripheral vision and sub-vocalisation exercise

1. Using the vertical hand motion:
2. Take the reading material chosen for the practise and begin reading by capturing 2 words at a time- mentally pronounce only one of the words- do this for one page.
3. Repeat but this time capture 3 words with each fixation, mentally pronounce only one of the words- do this for one page.
4. Repeat but this time capture half a line at a time and again mentally pronounce only one of the words- do this for one page.
5. **Now using the skimming hand motion:**
6. Repeat but this time capture two half lines at a time and again mentally pronounce only one of the words- do this for 2 pages.
7. Repeat but this time capture three half lines at a time and again mentally pronounce only one of the words- do this for 3 pages.
8. Repeat but this time capture five half lines at a time and again mentally pronounce only one of the words- do this for 5 pages.
9. Perform this exercise rhythmically, maintain the same pace throughout and ensure you stick to the amount of words per fixation as instructed.

Exercise 4- fixation training

1. Using a folded blank piece of paper that has the same width as half a line in your chosen reading material and the length of the folded paper should equal the height of the reading material.
2. Read the first half line of a page, then quickly cover that half line with the blank piece of paper and try to picture that half line on that blank page.
3. Proceed to the next half of the line, glance and then cover it- try and picture it on the blank paper.
4. Proceed to the next lines until you have completed 3 pages.
5. Then repeat for 3 pages capturing 2 half lines at a time- then visualising those two half lines on the blank paper.
6. Then repeat for 5 more pages this time capturing 3 half lines at a time.
7. Perform this exercise rhythmically and maintain the same smooth pace throughout.

Training schedule

1. Practise daily.
2. Cycle through the exercises with greater emphasis on the power exercises 1 and 2:
   a. Monday- exercise 1
   b. Tuesday- exercise 2
   c. Wednesday- exercise 3
   d. Thursday- exercise 4
   e. Friday- exercise 1
   f. Saturday- exercise 2
3. On Sunday, if time permits- perform a longer version of your favourite exercise- this can be done by multiplying the time of each step by a suitable factor, for example in exercise one-

we can multiply each step by 5, to make the first read through 25 minutes long, the second read through 20 minutes and so on.

Incorporating speed reading into daily life - crucial

The best way to master an important skill is through incorporation of the skill into your daily routine. For speed reading this could be done in the following ways:

1. Use the speed reading techniques in all that you read.
2. Develop one book a week habit- or at least aim for this target. Those who read more, become faster readers naturally.
3. Use your compulsory reading list (text books, memos, academic papers...etc) and practise your reading skills on them.
4. Practise layered reading at least once a week- be it on a whole book, a chapter or a long article.
5. Use layered reading for all your non-leisure reading materials.
6. **<u>Most importantly practise the drills daily.</u>**

Summary and Revision-Map

Key points

- Concentration is crucial for faster reading- hence regular practise of the techniques from earlier sections is important.
- Regressions should be minimised by centring attention prior to reading as well as using a guide (hand motion techniques) for pacing.
- Only 2 hand motion techniques should be used- "S" shape for skimming and vertical line for everything else.
- Sub-vocalisation needs to be minimised in order to break through to higher reading speeds.
- The number of words in each fixation needs to be expanded, but the time spent on each fixation should be maintained (and governed by the hand motion).
- Layered reading should be used for all study materials- this will improve reading speed, comprehension, long term recall and ease of study.
- Subconscious reading should be added to the layered reading procedure for a further improvement in comprehension.
- The practitioner should get comfortable with the technique and thereafter avoid any focus on it- dedicating the full attention to material being read.

Revision-Map

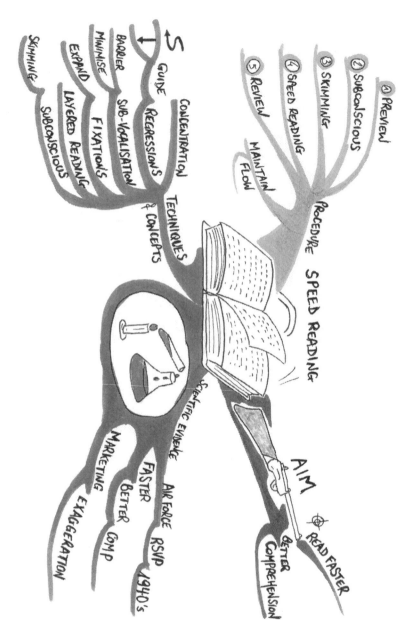

Part 4- Ultimate Study Method

What we learn with pleasure we never forget.

Alfred Mercier

Aims

- Master an efficient and effective structured approach to learning.
- Improve note taking and revision.
- Learn how to maintain the knowledge for long periods of time.

The Ultimate Study Method (USM)

The Ultimate Study Method (USM) that is introduced in this chapter gathers together all the topics exposed thus far in the book and combines them together to produce an optimal, enjoyable, efficient and effective approach to learning anything.

The key processes that occur when learning something new are as follows:

1. Go through the material.
2. Understand the material.
3. Memorise the understanding.
4. Review the memory to keep it fresh and promote long term retention.
5. Reinforce the information by using it to solve questions, problems, puzzles and games.
6. Build on the information by learning a new topic that uses what you have learnt as basics.

In order to arrive to stage (f) in the above list, it is necessary to have diligently gone through the previous stages on the same list. It becomes apparent that to truly expand one's knowledge, it is necessary to have an effective method to accumulate what has already been learnt into easily accessible long term memory- without this, further learning would be met with limitations due to a lack of basics.

The aim should be to keep anything that is of even mild importance in long term storage; this is feasible by following the system illustrated below. The greatest benefits will come when you realise that, the more you know and retain, the more easily you can learn new things and the more knowledge you can leverage on for the creation of new ideas as well as solving new problems.

Some recently began to argue that the need to maintain vast amounts of data in the brain has become redundant with the advent of easily accessible stores of digital data on the internet, which can be accessed in mere seconds by powerful search engines. This belief misses the point: information is of limited use when it is not reasoned out and clearly imprinted in the mind. For example, it would be very difficult for one to solve a problem whose concepts are so alien that he would not even know which search criteria to impose; even if the information was found, the reader's knowledge of the basics would not be sufficient to understand the procedure of the solution- it would be like learning physics in a foreign language (say in Aramaic).

When knowledge is reasoned out and then imprinted in the mind, it begins to overlap and interconnections are made- this is how creative new ideas come about. Having it reside in the digital world does not allow for that to happen. The accumulation of knowledge requires a certain critical mass before it becomes effective; if this stage is skipped, very few ideas are likely to come about. Perhaps the reader should notice how many truly revolutionary ideas have come about after the invention of the internet and compare them to the feats of the human mind that were attained beforehand. Perhaps when we get machines to connect between concepts and create new ones, knowledge accumulation would become redundant- though this would likely rob humanity of the joy of learning and creating; it would be the antithesis of most scholars Faustian tendencies.

The technique is easy to learn and comes naturally after very little practise. The overall procedure is as follows:

1. Gather all the material necessary for the completion of the study.
2. Enter a relaxed state of mind using one of the concentration exercises (Buddhist breathing is recommended- but stick to

whichever works best and whatever your environment or circumstances allow).

3. Use the Speed Reading technique in order to read through the material:
   a. Previewing
   b. Subconscious reading (optional)
   c. Skimming- After skimming begin to fill the main branches of the Revision-Map
   d. Speed reading-
      i. Speed read
      ii. Annotate difficult sections
      iii. Annotate key points
   e. Review
      i. Reason the topic
      ii. Complete Revision-Map
      iii. Complete linear notes
4. Memorise:
   a. Memorise the Revision-Map
   b. Review the Revision-Map
   c. Memorise the linear notes created, and
   d. Review the linear note.
5. Reinforce
   a. Games
   b. Puzzles
   c. Tests

The entire procedure forms the method: no steps should be skipped- it works best when it is followed according to the above prescription.

Key concepts

Concentration

Every study session should begin with a 5 minutes concentration exercise as was discussed in depth in the concentration section (Buddhist breathing is recommended but choose whichever works best for you).

The motivation behind this is to centre the mind and ensure that the entire study period is spent on the task at hand, avoiding distractions. This allows for a much better opportunity to understand the concepts being learnt and also increases the retention of information, since by concentration you are focusing your attention and attention is the key to memory.

As discussed in the concentration section, it is important to regularly practise the techniques as per the suggested schedule- a good grasp of the concentration techniques is an important ingredient of this system (this is why concentration is the first section of the book- everything follows from it).

Revision-Map

A Revision-Map is a pictorial representation of the topic; it is an extremely powerful tool to capture the structure of the topic as well as key facts.

Diagrammatic representations of topics and ideas have been used for centuries with notable examples including Porphyry of Tyros and Ramon Llull. Most recently, Tony Buzan's invention of Mind-Mapping, has improved the diagrammatic representation concept into a very specific methodology which transformed this general technique into a powerful tool for studying, brainstorming, lecturing, thinking, organising information, problem solving, decision making, and more. Tony Buzan's Mind Map book offers an excellent source of further information for the interested reader.

The pictorial representation of a topic has taken many names over the years: Cognitive Mapping, Mind Mapping, Concept Mapping, Mental Mapping, Spatial Organisation and others. However, in this book we will refer to the technique as Revision-Mapping- this is because the USM mainly uses this approach as a revision tool for long term memory storage.

A Revision-Map forms a key component in the Ultimate Study Method, since such a succinct representation of the topic offers a very quick review of what has been learnt; and thus it is the instrument we use to solicit long term memory storage. Apart from that, creating a Revision-Map forces the user to think about the overall structure of the topic and how different elements are related-this improves understanding and assimilation of the knowledge.

The list of advantages is as follows:

1. Succinct representation, which is useful for long term memory storage- this is the main motivation for using the Revision-Map.
2. Forces one to think about how the different concepts are related- improves understanding and assimilation.
3. Synoptic representation of the topic.
4. Uses both brain hemispheres when creating the Revision-Map forces more involvement in the reasoning of the topic.
5. Can organise large amounts of information in a form that provides a better platform for reasoning.
6. The concept is very natural and is similar to the way in which the brain links information.
7. Enhances creativity.

The Ultimate Study Method uses Revision-Maps in a very specific manner; it is important to note that Revision-Maps are not the only notes being created in this study method- we use linear note taking as well. The Revision-Maps are used to provide a structural representation that is easy to review for long term memory creation, whilst the linear notes provide a more complete coverage of all the elements in the topic. **Linear notes are absolutely necessary,** since a Revision-Map on its own cannot capture some of the subtleties that need to be explained in worded form. Neither linear notes nor Revision-Maps are necessarily better than the other; they complement each other- **both must** be used since the purposes that each serves are different.

The procedure for Revision-Mapping is as follows:

1. Begin at the centre of a blank page- draw an image representing the topic.
2. From the main image draw branches that represent the key divisions of the topic.
3. On each branch write the key word representing the concept.
   a. Branches should only be as long as the keywords.
   b. Use only the keywords, nothing else- do not include sentences or explanations.
   c. If there is an image that represents the keyword well then use the image instead of the keyword. (When Revision-Mapping, images are preferred to words)
   d. If the image only reminds you of the keyword, then put both on the branch to avoid confusion when interpreting.
   e. A powerful approach is to use the image as the branch and put the keyword on top of it (see for example the Revision-Maps in this book).
4. You can then divide the subject into its subdivisions by drawing branches from each key word.

a. The Branches should be thickest near the centre and become thinner as you branch out- so the main key division of the topic will have thick branches whilst the sub division will have thinner ones and so on.

b. Continue using keywords only- one key word per branch.

c. Use images instead of keywords where the image interpretation is obvious, otherwise use both- if there is no image that comes to mind then do not put an image- it is not compulsory only an added bonus.

5. Use boxes to contain items that are not keywords- for example, key formulae should be in boxes next to the keyword that describes them.

6. Continue until the main themes and concepts have been exposed on the single page.

7. General considerations:

a. Do not spend much time on making the images perfect- it is not necessary. Simply ensure that the image represents the concept you wanted to portray and then move on.

b. Use a colouring scheme- each main branch sets the colour for that entire division- so for example, if the topic can be divided into 5 key divisions, you will use 5 colours- each division's branches are painted with just one, staying consistent and ensuring that subdivisions are painted with the same colour as the main division from which it branches out.

c. Use black ink for writing the keywords (irrespective of the colour of the branch- keywords and formulae are all written in black ink).

d. Use capital letters for the keywords- this takes little extra effort but makes the review quicker.

e. Use arrows to connect related concepts that are on different branches.

f. Ensure the Revision-Map is clear, concise and well organised.

     g. Work clockwise.

8. Spend some time looking at others' Revision-Maps to see examples and generate ideas.

9. With time and experimentation, settle on your own personal style, but ensure the main guidelines above are adhered to.

In this book, at the end of every chapter there is a Revision-Map summarising the concepts of the chapter. These should provide good examples as to how a Revision-Map should look like. Remember, the emphasis is not on artistic prowess, but on a synoptic exposition of the main concepts- you should not compete with others in making "better, nicer and prettier" Revision-Maps, the main goal is to develop an effective tool for quickly reviewing the topic.

Linear Notes

Linear notes are the traditional way in which a topic is summarised. With the recent emerging popularity of Revision-Maps, fewer people are relying on linear note taking. Such an approach is flawed since Revision-Maps are not sufficient for covering all the concepts in a topic.

The aim of linear note taking is to capture, in your own words, all the concepts of a topic. For example, when reading through a text book, the linear notes should cover all the main concepts covered in the textbook but with brief explanations rather than full analysis. The rules for linear note taking are as follows:

1. All the concepts of the topic should be covered.

2. Each concept should be summarised, using your own words- this requires first reasoning the concept discussed and then writing down this understanding in your own words- as briefly as possible- the key motivation is to have a concise record to which you can later refer to in order to immediately

remind yourself of the understanding you already arrived at in the past.

3. Try to explain each concept in one paragraph or less- ideally less than or equal to 3 lines.
4. Stick to a hierarchical structure as follows:
   a. Each main division should be underlined with a double line.
   b. Each sub division should be underlined with a single line.
   c. Each concept:
      i. Should begin with a bullet point.
      ii. The keyword describing the concept.
      iii. The explanation of the concept.
      iv. A list of sub components (if any), each beginning with a hyphen or roman numerals if order is important.
      v. Include diagrams and formulae under the concept- ensure these are surrounded by boxes.
5. General considerations
   i. Use black ink.
   ii. Underline important keywords in the explanation (do not over do this- underline only 1-2 words at a time).
   iii. The organisation of the notes should be in the form you think is best- it does not necessarily have to be in the order chosen by the author/lecturer of the book or topic.

The following is a generic example:

Book/topic Title

<u>Division heading 1</u>

<u>Sub-division Heading 1</u>

- Keyword 1- explanation
- Keyword 2- explanation

> Formula

- Keyword 3- explanation

    -subcomponent 1

    -subcomponent 2

- Keyword 4- explanation

    i.   Ordered fact 1
    ii. Ordered fact 2
    iii. Ordered fact 3
    iv. Etc...

<u>Sub-division Heading 2</u>
Etc...

- Keyword 4- explanation
- Keyword 5- explanation
- Keyword 6- explanation

<u>Division heading 2</u>

<u>Sub-division Heading 1</u>

Etc...

The linear notes should be used to initially learn, understand and reason the topic; it is necessary to read through these notes several times until the topic is absolutely clear in the mind. Once the topic is clear and all the facts have been memorised, it is only necessary to go through the linear notes again during the specified review periods (see memorisation section).

Unique identifiers

As explained in the memory section of this manual; using unique identifiers allows the user to systematically break down the subject into main components which are then memorised consistently- this avoids confusion and offers the most efficient approach for later recall.

The list of identifiers should include all the main items that would need to be memorised and the corresponding images that would be used for each identifier. Using the example from the math subsection in the chapter on memory:

Symbol	Image	Why
+	Pus	Plus sounds like Pus
-	Dennis the Menace	Minus sounds like Menace
=	Eagle	Equal sounds like Eagle
2π	Two pies	Since the letter is pi and there are two
μ	A cow	Since the letter is pronounced mu
$\sqrt{}$	Root	Since it is the square root symbol
( )	Twin Towers	Since visually it looks like two towers
σ	Sigmund Freud	Since the letter is pronounced Sigma
Division	Machete	Division is associated with cutting...
Power	Bodybuilder	Power associated with muscles
Integration	Interrogation light	Integration sounds like interrogation
Differentiation	Sock	Differentiating between the pairs of socks

These symbols appear in a large variety of mathematical formulae; hence, providing an image for each in advance makes the process of memorising formulae quicker, easier and without conflict or confusion. The list should then be extended as and when new symbols are encountered repeatedly, and thus need to be anchored to one image which can be used to represent them going forward.

The length of the list would depend on the size of the topic and the number of key components (which repeatedly feature in the topic) to which it can be broken down into.

It is essential to be consistent across topics; so for example, if you were studying physics as well as mathematics, you would be using the same table above for both and only adding to the list components that are not already included.

Advantages of taking an organised approach with key identifiers:

1. Systematically breaks down the topics into key components.
2. There is no confusion of using the same image twice or having two images representing the same concept.
3. It makes memorisation of other topics with similar identifiers much easier (e.g. physics and maths).
4. It provides a reference in case an image for an identifier was forgotten.

Speed reading

The Speed Reading technique should be performed as instructed in the Speed Reading chapter. The main additional points to be made are regarding the annotation of the material as you read through it and the reasoning of the topic. The key to the system is to have a continuous flow through the data, avoiding any stopping and frustrations early in the reading process- this should be performed using the following approach:

1. When reading through difficult concepts that are not clear as you pass through them, annotate the margin of the line the concept is on with a question mark.
2. When reading through key concepts that should be memorised, simply annotate the margin with a "V" (avoid underlying or using highlighters at this stage; the aim is to go through the information without stopping for long- underlying can be used later when forming the linear notes).
3. On subsequent reads through the data, if the points that caused confusion have been understood, simply put a "V" next to the question mark.
4. Do not stop to reason any difficult point, the aim is to flow through the data smoothly and continuously- this way, key concepts are picked up and then further details are accumulated as you fill the gaps in subsequent reads.

5. Reasoning through anything that remains unclear is done at the stage of note taking.

Combining these key points with the speed reading method, we arrive at the following procedure for the reading stage in the USM:

1. Previewing
2. Subconscious reading (optional)
3. Skimming- After skimming, begin to fill the main branches of the Revision-Map.
4. Speed reading-
   a. While speed reading, annotate the text using a red pen.
   b. Put a question mark at the beginning of a line that contains a concept you do not understand.
   c. Put a "V" next to concepts that are very important and that you would like to take away from this source.
   d. Add to the Revision-Map key concepts that were covered and annotated during this speed reading phase.
5. Review
6. Skim through the text again but this time slow down at any point that has a question mark next to it- **but do not stop**; simply read at a slower rate and put a "V" next to the question mark if the concept was understood after this read through. If, after this second read through the material the point is still not understood, keep reading on (do not stop) and come back to it on the next step of the review.
7. Begin writing your linear notes- these should contain all the main points of the topic in your own words; so go through the text again ensuring that every concept that is annotated as important has been included. When writing these notes, spend whatever time necessary to reason the topic, it is at this point that you can stop at parts that have not been understood in earlier reading through the material. Reason the topic so

that it is fully understood and write down the key concepts in your own words.

8. Add to the Revision-Map all the extra key concepts gleaned from the second part of the review.

Memorising

Memorising the topic follows 3 stages:

1. Memorise the Revision-Map- to get an overall understanding of the topic and have a structure on to which you can attach further knowledge.
2. Memorise the linear notes- adding on to the general structure gained by memorising the Revision-Map- this procedure adds finer details.
3. Review.
4. Review the linear notes using the optimal review windows.
5. Review the Revision-Maps every other day- this is for the purpose of long term memory storage.

Out of the 3 stages above, it is usually the last stage (Review) that tends to be neglected the most. Long term retention of the data relies on periodic review- without doing this, all the efforts of learning and memorising a topic will be lost.

In order to be efficient, we review according to the optimal review periods (which are determined by the "forgetting curves" theory), so that we only do what is necessary for long term retention without overdoing it and thus wasting time.

When memorising the Revision-Map and the linear notes, the most appropriate memory method should be used for each portion. For example, any formula should be memorised with the approach demonstrated in the math section of the memory chapter, whilst any word definition should be memorised using the method that was applied to foreign vocabulary (as demonstrated in the memory chapter). The key is to be systematic in the approach and to ensure the unique identifiers list is updated with any new components as you progress through the topic.

The overall aim should be to memorise the Revision-Map in its entirety and to memorise just the key facts from the linear notes. This way the structure of the topic is embedded in the mind and the facts relating to the structure are immediately available.

Note that the linear notes are there to provide a full coverage of the topic, but presented in a terser form and in your own words- it is there to allow you to reason through the topic, have a complete reference and contain all the key facts. It is not necessary to memorise it word for word- only key facts and principles.

Memorising the Revision-Map:

1. The recommended approach is to use either the link system or the loci system, under the following considerations:
   a. In the link system, each key concept is linked to the concepts that are connected to it in a clockwise direction. So you begin with the innermost concept, link the key ideas on its branches in clockwise direction, then repeat the procedure for each of the key concepts and the ideas on their respective branches, until the entire Revision-Map has been memorised.
   b. Using the loci system involves using (or creating) a town for studying; each house (home, building, or other establishment) in the town represents one topic. Each room in the house represents the key ideas, and each item in the room represents the sub branches etc.
   c. The link system is generally recommended because it is a powerful way to later connect between topics; since all

knowledge eventually overlaps, such an approach seems quite natural.

2. Review the links created above using the optimal revision periods at the very least:

   a. Review the Revision-Map every time you review the linear notes.

   b. In addition, and since the Revision-Map is so short and concise- it is recommended to review the Revision-Map every other day.

   c. With time, as you perform this for more topics, you will have many such Revision-Maps- by that time, you would have grown so comfortable with each of the old ones that it would take less than a minute to go through each one. That would mean that you could easily keep 30 topics fresh in the mind, whilst spending less than 30 minutes every other day.

   d. It is strongly recommended to follow these guidelines; the extra time taken will ensure the topics that you have spent so much time and effort learning do not get pruned as your brain clears memories that are not necessary for long term storage. The few minutes spent every other day are worth it, and since you would be going through the ludicrous links you created to memorise the topic, this should actually be a pleasurable experience.

3. It is strongly recommended to create a list of unique identifiers, as was done in the memory section; the key is to have a unique identifier for each important data type that is repeated frequently in the topic. For example, for a math topic, it would be a list of symbols, letters and functions with their corresponding unique image (keep this list separate from the notes). The advantages of doing this are:

   a. It is useful as a reference when reviewing this topic.

   b. It is also useful for easier memorisation of similar topics in the future.

    c. It reduces confusion, since you avoid using different images for the same concept or one image for 2 different concepts.

Memorising the linear notes:

1. Read through the notes a couple of times to make sure that everything has been clearly understood.
2. It is not necessary to memorise it word for word- only the key principles should be memorised.
3. Break down the data into key components and add to the list of unique identifiers. Memorise using the techniques introduced in the memory section. Notice that it is **not necessary** to memorise the structure of the linear notes (i.e. heading->sub heading->fact); just memorise the facts, as the structure was already memorised with the Revision-Map.
4. Review- this is extremely important:
       a. After memorising the data with the techniques above (this is time = T_0), repeat the scene or image in your mind straight after, to ensure the data has been absorbed.
       b. An hour later ($T_0 + 1$hour), attempt to recall the data and review the scene/image.
       c. A couple of hours before going to bed, that is, $T_0 + 12$hours, (assuming the data was learnt in the day, otherwise simply perform 12 hours later) review again.
       d. Review again the next day (i.e. $T_0 + 24$ hours).
       e. Review once more a week later (i.e. $T_0 + 1$ Week).
       f. Review once more 2 weeks later (i.e. $T_0 + 2$ Weeks).
       g. Review once more 1 month later (i.e. $T_0 + 1$ month).
       h. Review once more 3 months later (i.e. $T_0 + 3$ months).
       i. Review once more 6 months later (i.e. $T_0 + 6$ months).
       j. Review once more 12 months later (i.e. $T_0 + 12$ months).

Reinforce

You learn best by doing!

This is especially true for problem solving and logical thinking-related tasks. Tests that simply involve recall do not require this, but tests that involve the need to understand the topic make this point crucial.

Make it fun:

    a. Solve exercises related to the topic (exam questions, riddles, puzzles, text book questions...etc).
    b. Play games related to the topic if any exist.
    c. Build/create by using the principles of the topic (e.g. computer programming).
    d. Watch movies or read other books related to the topic if any exist.
    e. Join forums debating the topic.

Overall

Overall your notes should consist of the following:

    1. Revision-Map
    2. List of unique identifiers
    3. Linear notes

It is recommended to photocopy (or to scan into PDF format) the Revision-Map of each topic, and then create a folder (or PDF file) with all the Revision-Maps of all the topics memorised to date. The aim is to then review all the Revision-Maps every other day. The recommended approach is to master one topic at a time and review the Revision-Map every other day. By the time you begin learning a new topic, the previous topic's Revision-Map is so fresh in the mind that it only takes 1-2 minutes to go through it in its entirety. By the time the second topic has been learnt, there are 2 Revision-Maps, and each should take 1-2 minutes to review; and this should still be done every other day.

As time goes by, this repeated use will ensure the settlement of the topic into long term memory storage. By then, going through each Revision-Map would take even less time, and so 20-30 different topics can quite easily be reviewed in a period of 30 minutes. This only needs to be done every other day and is a small price to pay for long term retention of data- the benefits far outweigh the "cost" and using funny memory links makes this process very enjoyable.

A very interesting event will occur after sufficient review: the information will be so clear in one's mind that the physical notes will not be necessary when reviewing- it will all be done mentally. Such reviews are extremely quick; a topic can be covered in less than a minute and it is a very satisfying level of mastery to achieve, which will provide a great deal of confidence in one's knowledge of the subjects involved. It would also provide confidence in the study technique, as well as one's own natural capacity for learning.

For completeness, the overall procedure is as follows:

1. Gather all the material necessary for the completion of the study.
2. Enter a **relaxed** state of mind, using one of the concentration exercises (Buddhist breathing is recommended- but stick to whichever works best for you and whatever your environment or circumstances allow).
3. Use the **Speed Reading** technique in order to read through the material:
   a. Previewing
   b. Subconscious reading (optional)

c. Skimming- After skimming, begin to fill the main branches of the Revision-Map.

d. Speed reading-

    i. While speed reading, annotate the text using a red pen.

    ii. Put a question mark at the beginning of a line that contains a concept you do not understand.

    iii. Put a "V" next to concepts that are very important and that you would like to take away from this source.

    iv. Add to the Revision-Map key concepts that were covered and annotated during this speed reading phase.

e. Review

    i. Skim through the text again but this time slow down at any point that has a question mark next to it- **but do not stop**; simply read at a slower rate and put a "V" next to the question mark if the point was understood. If, after this second read through the material, the point is still not understood, keep reading on (do not stop) and come back to it on the next step of the review.

    ii. Begin writing your linear notes- these should contain all the main points of the topic in your own words; so go through the text again, ensuring every concept that is annotated as important has been included. When writing these notes, spend whatever time necessary to reason the topic; it is at this phase that you can stop at points that have not been understood in earlier readings through the material. Reason the topic so that it is fully understood and write down the key concepts in your own words.

    iii. Add to the Revision-Map all the extra key concepts gleaned from the second part of the review.

4. **Memorise the Revision-Map:**

a. The recommended approach is to use either the link system or the loci system.

    i. In the link system, each key concept is linked to the concepts that are connected to it in a clockwise direction. So you begin with the innermost concept, link the key ideas on its branches in clockwise direction, then repeat the procedure for each of the key concepts and the ideas on their respective branches, until the entire Revision-Map has been memorised.

    ii. Using the loci system involves using (or creating) a town for studying; then each house (home, building, or other establishment) in the town represents one topic. Each room in the house represents the key ideas, and each item in the room represents the sub branches etc.

    iii. The link system is generally recommended because it is a powerful way to later connect between topics; since all knowledge eventually overlaps- such an approach seems quite natural.

b. Review the links created above, using the optimal revision periods at the very least:

    i. So review the Revision-Map every time you review the linear notes.

    ii. In addition, and since the Revision-Map is so short and concise- it is recommended to review the Revision-Map every other day.

    iii. With time, as you perform this for more topics, you will have many such Revision-Maps- by that time, you would have grown so comfortable with each of the old ones that it would take less than a minute to go through each one. That would mean that you could easily keep 30 topics fresh in the mind, whilst spending less than 30 minutes every other day.

    iv. It is strongly advised to follow these guidelines- the extra time taken will ensure that the topics you have spent so much time and effort learning do not get pruned as your brain clears memories that are not necessary for long term storage. The few minutes spent every other day are worth it, and since you would be going through the ludicrous links you created to memorise the topic, this should actually be a pleasurable experience.

  c. It is strongly recommended to create a list of unique identifiers, as was done in the memory section- the key is to have a unique identifier for each important data type that is repeated in the topic. For example, for a math topic it would be a list of symbols, letters and functions with their corresponding unique image (keep this list separate from the notes). The advantages of doing this are:

    i. This is useful as a reference when reviewing this topic.

    ii. It is also useful for easier memorisation of future similar topics.

    iii. It reduces confusion, since you avoid using different images for the same concept or one image for 2 different concepts.

5. **Memorise the linear notes** created

6. Read through the notes a couple of times to make sure that everything has been clearly understood.

7. It is not necessary to memorise it word for word- only the key principles should be memorised.

8. Break down the data into key components and add to the list of unique identifiers. Memorise using the techniques introduced in the memory section. Notice that it is **not necessary** to memorise the structure here (i.e. heading->sub heading->fact); just memorise the facts, as the structure was already memorised with the Revision-Map.

9. Review- this is extremely important:
    a. After memorising the data with the techniques above (this is time = T_0), repeat the scene or image in your mind straight after, to ensure the data has been absorbed.
    b. An hour later (T_0 + 1hour), attempt to recall the data and review the scene/image.
    c. A couple of hours before going to bed, that is, T_0 + 12hours, (assuming the data was learnt in the day, otherwise simply perform 12 hours later) review again.
    d. Review again the next day (i.e. T_0 + 24 hours).
    e. Review once more a week later (i.e. T_0 + 1 Week).
    f. Review once more 2 weeks later (i.e. T_0 + 2 Weeks).
    g. Review once more 1 month later (i.e. T_0 + 1 month).
    h. Review once more 3 months later (i.e. T_0 + 3 months).
    i. Review once more 6 months later (i.e. T_0 + 6 months).
    j. Review once more 12 months later (i.e. T_0 + 12 months).
10. **Reinforce**:
    a. Solve exercises relating to the topic (exam questions, riddles, puzzles, text book questions...etc).
    b. Play games related to the topic, if any exist.
    c. Build or create using the principles of the topic.
    d. Watch movies or read other books related to the topic, if any exist.

Summary and Revision-Map

Key points

- The USM builds on all the concepts introduced in this book.
- A summary of the overall procedure is as follows:
    a. Gather Materials.
    b. Deepen state of mind.
    c. Speed Reading procedure (preview, skim, speed read, review):
        i. Flow, do not stop!
        ii. Annotate difficult sections with "?".
        iii. Annotate important sections with "V".
        iv. Complete the Revision-Map.
        v. Complete the linear notes.
    d. Reason and understand the topic.
    e. Memorise the Revision-Map and linear notes.
    f. Review the linear notes according to the optimal revision periods.
    g. Review the Revision-Map every other day.
    h. Reinforce by using and extending the knowledge gained.

- Unique identifiers should be created if the topic is novel, or should be borrowed if available from a similar topic.
- Revision-Maps provide structural depiction as well as a succinct representation of the topic.
- Linear notes provide a terser yet full coverage of the topic in the practitioner's own words.
- Revision-Maps and linear notes must be used together; neither is sufficient on its own.
- Review is crucial for long term retention.

Revision Map

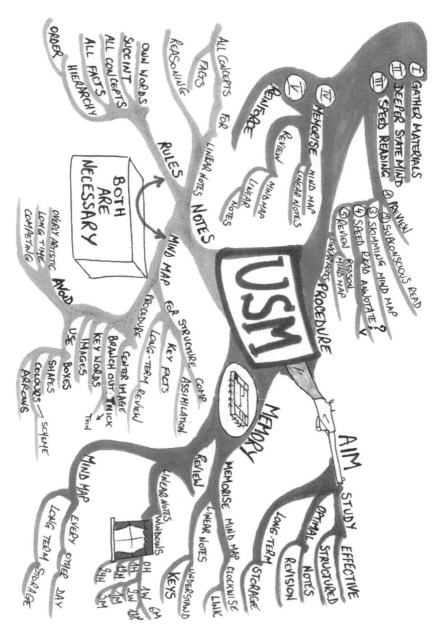

Part 5- Rapid math

Mathematics is the queen of sciences and arithmetic is the queen of mathematics

Carl Friedrich Gauss

Aims

- Improve the ability to use and understand numbers in daily life.
- Reduce the need for a calculator or machine-assisted thinking which slows down the thought process.
- Practise your memory skills.
- Challenge and exercise the brain.

Mental arithmetic

Using the mind to perform calculations is an extremely powerful tool for keeping the mind sharp. When performing mental arithmetic, one first needs to be able to visualise the numbers in the mind's eye; then there is a need to decide on the optimal approach for the calculation, which is followed by performing the logical manipulations mentally, whilst simultaneously memorising each digit of the result; the procedure is then completed by recalling the result from memory. Having the arithmetic procedure broken down in this manner illustrates the faculties required and exercised during the calculation process. Mental calculations test one's memory and concentration abilities to their extremes- it is a very good all-round brain exercise.

Apart from keeping the mind sharp, another advantage of mental arithmetic mastery is that, by being able to calculate mentally, the train of thought is rarely disrupted by the need to reach out to a calculator, phone or computer in order to find a result from which further thinking can follow. The ability to do so is crucial for some jobs more than others; it is especially important where quick decision making is a necessary skill for remaining profitable. Professional financial market trading is a typical example but physical goods market vendors or other hagglers also tend to have excellent arithmetic skills.

Becoming proficient at mental calculation will provide an insight into the world of numbers and set a corner stone over which more abstract thinking can be placed with sounder footing.

With arithmetic, examples are a crucial part of learning- the reader is advised to follow the examples closely until the logic is clearly understood.

World Records

Category	Result	Record holder	Year
Multiply two 13-digit numbers correctly	28 seconds	Shakuntala Devi	1980
Addition of ten 10-digit numbers correctly	3m19s	Marc Jornet Sanz	2010
Extracting the square root of a 6 digit number to 8dp correctly	6m19s	Selçuk Soner Akgül	2010

Scientific Evidence

Mental calculators were investigated scientifically as early as 1894; Alfred Binet discovered that such individuals had an amazing ability to remember complex sequences of numbers. Ericson and Kintsch (1995) then suggested that such fascination with a topic makes one create retrieval structures that enable recall of complex sequences or components of the topic- this has been proposed as a theory to explain Alfred Binet's discovery.

Functional Neuroimaging research suggests that the parietal brain circuits facilitate arithmetic problem-solving and that the use of the circuits change with training. Individuals with higher mathematical abilities were shown to display stronger activation of the left angular gyrus while solving arithmetic problems.

Research on the development of children as well as adult performance with training have shown that the activation of the circuits of the brain that are crucial for mathematical skills can change with training, experience and developmental growth. In 2003, Delazer et al. have shown that adults that received training in arithmetic problem-solving have shown higher activation of the left angular gyrus relative to adults that did not receive such training.

Additional testing on abacus experts have shown that, through intensive training and practise, their neural pathways have connected more effectively for the purposes of arithmetic, thus resulting in exceptional calculation abilities.

The majority of the scientific evidence suggests that, with training, mental arithmetic abilities can be activated and improved in most cases. The added advantage of activating the aforementioned parts of the brain is that the effects spill-over to other mathematical skills and problem solving abilities.

Techniques

This section introduces the techniques that form the system for mental arithmetic; only the optimal methods are introduced- the focus is on efficiency and pragmatism rather than a complete exposition of all the tricks. It is the author's belief that knowing lots of tricks that should be used under different scenarios forces the practitioner to spend valuable time viewing the problem in search of the right technique, instead of using this time to actually solve. Familiarity with a couple of optimal tricks combined with the powerful general technique appears to offer better performance overall.

Therefore, the exposition of this chapter focuses on each arithmetic function, the main technique used to solve as well as selected powerful tricks that complement the overall approach.

Addition

We begin by exploring the simplest of arithmetic operations. The approach taken is simple and applied equally to all addition problems. The procedure is as follows:

1. If the numbers are not written on paper, memorise them as they are being read out (once you become proficient, you can simply add them along as each one is being read to you) - if they are written down, this step is not necessary.
2. Mentally align all numbers to the rightmost margin.
3. Begin at the rightmost column- add all the numbers together.
4. Proceed to the next column (working from right to left) and add the numbers to the second digit (if any, zero otherwise) of the result from step (3).

5. Memorise the last two digits of the result- use the link system, link this first result to "pus". If the result is only one digit, then add a zero to its left.

6. Repeat the procedure by going down the third column but add the remainder (the leftmost digit of the result from (4) if there were 3 digits- zero otherwise).

7. Continue by memorising two digits of the result every time, whilst carrying the remainder, if any, to the next column. Link each two digits to the image of the previous two digits.

Example 1- Add 4567 to 8977

Begin by writing down the numbers vertically (there is no need to write down any of the work- it should all be done mentally):

$$\begin{array}{r} 4567 \\ + \quad 8977 \\ \hline \end{array}$$

- Begin by adding the rightmost digits: 7+7=14.
- Next, add the digits in the next column (2nd from the right) to the second column of the result already obtained (14) - so this gives 144.
- Memorise 44 as the rightmost part of the solution and carry the remainder to the next column- the image may be something like: "a lion made out of pus is roaring".
- Add the remainder carried to the third column's first digit (5) - so 5+1=6, then add to this the next digits in this column (9) - so 6+9=15.
- Proceed as before to the next column and add the digits of the column to the second digit of our result so far (15) - so adding the 4 we get 55 and adding the 8 we get 135.

- This is the final portion of the result- memorise this number by linking its image to the previous image (lion) – perhaps link mule (35) to lion and tie (1) to mule.

It is now simple to recall the result- think of "pus" and you get the result from right to left (or think of tie as you finish the calculation and you get the result from left to right):

Result =13,544

Example 2- add 135,897 + 448,185 + 399,407 + 915,323 + 466

We begin the exposition by writing out the problem with right side alignment:

$$
\begin{array}{r}
135,897 \\
448,185 \\
399,407 \\
915,323 \\
+ \quad\quad 466 \\
\hline
\end{array}
$$

- Add the rightmost column to get 28.
- Move to the second column (2nd from the right) and add to the second digit of 28: so adding the 9 gives 118, adding the 8 gives 198, adding the zero gives 198, adding the 2 gives 218, and finally adding the 6 gives 278.
- Link 78 (coffee) to pus and carry 2 to the next column.
- Add the carried 2 to the first digit in the 3 column- so 2 +8=10, and then proceed to adding the digits in the column: 10+1=11, 11+4=15, 15+3=18 and 18+4=22.
- Proceed to the next column and add the digits in this column to the second digit of 22- so adding the 5 gives 72, adding the 8 gives 152, adding the 9 gives 242, and adding the 5 gives 292.

- Link 92 (bone) to 78 and carry 2.
- Add the carried 2 to the next column- so 2+3=5, 5+4=9, 9+9=18 and 18+1=19.
- Proceed to the final column and add the digits to the second digit of 19- so adding 1 gives 29, adding 4 gives 69, adding 3 gives 99, and adding 9 gives 189.
- Link 189 (tie, fob) to 92 (bone).

Result= 1,899,278

Example 3- in this example we demonstrate what to do when there is nothing to carry:

$$\begin{array}{r} 1,234,501 \\ 98,415,200 \\ 874,521,898,700 \\ 2,465,001 \\ +\quad 54,877,775,600 \\ \hline \end{array}$$

- Adding the rightmost column we get 2; since this is only one digit, we add a zero in the front of the two to get 02.
- Proceed by adding the second column to the second digit of 02 (i.e. the zero)- since the entire second column consists of zeros- the result is 02.
- Link 02 to pus- perhaps think of sun (**sun**=02) that has pus instead of rays.
- Proceed with the third column- sum the numbers to get 20, then go to the fourth column and add the digits of the column to the second digit of the result (i.e. 2)- so we get 290.
- Link the image of 90 to sun and carry the remainder (2) to the next column.

- Continue for the rest of the columns- note that an empty cell means zero- for example the eighth column has the numbers 0, 9, 2, 0, 7.

Result= 929,501,789,002

It is recommended to begin practising the technique by writing down the problem in the format used for the examples; only write down the problem, the solution should still be done in your head. As you become more proficient, you can simply add the numbers in your mind as they are being called out, or you can memorise the list of numbers in your mind and do the sum mentally without visual aid. It is recommended to begin practising with small numbers- say 3 numbers with 3 digits. After a little practise, increase the complexity by adding more numbers with more digits; there really is no limit- you can in fact add up in your mind more than what your calculator or Microsoft excel can handle. For example try adding the following numbers on your calculator or excel:

4565897987056132165798+25648912303548943152

The numbers will just get rounded up (Excel has a 15 digit precision) and the result provided will not be accurate to the nearest integer, however, in your mind, you can perform this quickly and precisely.

Multiplication

Unlike with addition, when performing multiplication, we first check to see whether simple tricks can simplify the calculation and, if so, we use them; if not, we proceed by applying the main method which can be used for any multiplication problem. The overall consideration procedure should be as follows:

1. Are both numbers close to the nearest 100? e.g. 107x103 or 89x92.
2. If so, use the tricks below.
3. If not, use the main method.

Tricks

If both numbers in the problem are close the nearest 100, then the following trick makes the multiplication much simpler. The procedure is as follows:

1. Are both numbers over the nearest hundred? If so,
   a. Take the amount by which one of the numbers is over the nearest hundred and add it to the other number in the problem- this is the left part of your answer (link the image of this number to multiplex-cinema- which is the image word for multiply).
   b. Take the amount by which each number is over the nearest hundred and multiply them together- this is the right side of your answer.
   c. Connect the left and right side of your answer- if the right side has more than 2 digits add these to the left result.
2. Are both numbers below the nearest hundred? If so,
   a. Take the amount by which one of the numbers is below the nearest hundred and subtract it from the other number in the problem- this is the left part of your answer (link

the image of this number to multiplex-cinema- which is the image word for multiply).

b. Take the amount by which each number is below the nearest hundred and multiply them together- this is the right side of your answer.

c. Connect the left and right side of your answer- if the right side has more than 2 digits add these to the left result.

3. Is one number below the nearest hundred whilst the other is over? If so,

a. Take the amount by which one of the numbers is over the nearest hundred and add it to the other number in the problem- this is the left part of your answer (link the image of this number to multiplex-cinema- which is the image word for multiply).

b. Take the amount by which each number is away from the nearest hundred and multiply them together.

c. Multiply your left hand side by 100 and deduct the result obtained in (b).

d. What results is the answer.

(Please note that both numbers have to be over or below the same 100)

As always, the best demonstration is through examples:

Example 1:

$$
\begin{array}{r}
104 \\
\times \quad 103 \\
\hline
\end{array}
$$

- The numbers are both over 100 so we can apply this technique.
- The amounts by which the numbers are over 100 are: 4 and 3.

- Adding 3 to 104 or adding 4 to 103 gives 107 => this is the left part of the answer. At this stage, it may be a good idea to memorise this number by linking its image to a multiplex cinema (multiply sounds a little like multiplex and the latter can be visualised easily) - going forward, all multiplication linking will be done to the image of a multiplex cinema. In the case of 107, the image of "desk" (**desk**=107) could be linked.
- Now multiply the amount by which each number is over 100- i.e. multiply 3x4 =12; this is the right side of the answer- since it is only 2 digits long there is no need for carrying over.
- The answer is therefore 107&12= 10,712.

Example 2:

$$
\begin{array}{r}
111 \\
\times \ \underline{112}
\end{array}
$$

- The numbers are both over 100 so we can proceed with the technique.
- The amounts by which the numbers are over 100 are: 11 and 12.
- Add either 11 to 112 or add 12 to 111 (it does not matter which you do) - both give 123 => this is the left part of the answer. Link it to multiplex cinema.
- Now multiply the amount by which each number is over 100 - i.e. multiply 11x12 =132; this is the right side of the answer, but since it is 3 digits long we need to add any digits beyond the second digit to the left side of the answer. In the case of 132 we therefore split the number into 1&32; 1 is added to the left side of the answer and 32 remains the right side of the answer.

- So 123 +1 =124 => this is the left side of the answer and the right side is 32.
- The answer is therefore 124&32= 12,432.

Example 3:

$$98$$
$$\text{x} \quad 91$$

- The numbers are both below 100 so we can proceed with the technique.
- The amounts by which the numbers are below 100 are: 2 and 9.
- Subtracting either 2 from 91 or 9 from 98 (it does not matter which you do) - both give 89 => this is the left part of the answer. Link it to multiplex cinema.
- Now multiply the amount by which each number is below 100 - i.e. multiply 2x9 =18; this is the right side of the answer and since it is only 2 digits long there is no need to carry a remainder.
- The answer is therefore 89&18= 8,918.

Example 4:

$$87$$
$$\text{x} \quad 89$$

- The numbers are both below 100 so we can proceed with the technique.

- The amounts by which the numbers are below 100 are: 13 and 11.
- Subtracting either 13 from 89 or 11 from 87 (it does not matter which you do) both give 76 => this is the left part of the answer. Link it to multiplex cinema.
- Now multiply the amount by which each number is below 100- i.e. multiply 11x13 =143; this is the right side of the answer- since it is 3 digits long we need to add any digits beyond the second digit to the left side of the answer. In the case of 143 we therefore split the number into 1&43; 1 is added to the left side of the answer and 43 remains the right side of the answer.
- The left hand side of the answer becomes 76+1=77.
- The answer is therefore 77&43= 7,743.

Example 5: Extensions to larger numbers

$$
\begin{array}{r}
912 \\
\times \quad 903 \\
\hline
\end{array}
$$

- The numbers are both over the nearest "100" (note that in this case the nearest 100 is 900) so we can apply this technique.

(Please note that both numbers have to be over the same 100- so if it was 812x903 the trick would not work, since one is over 800 whilst the other is over 900)

- The amounts by which the numbers are over the nearest 100 are: 12 and 3.
- Adding 3 to 912 or adding 12 to 903 gives 915.
- Since the nearest 100 which the two numbers are over is 900 we need to multiply the result by 9- so we calculate 915x9=8,235.

=> This is the left part of the answer. Link it to multiplex cinema.

- Now multiply the amount by which each number is over the nearest 100- i.e. multiply 3x12 =36; this is the right side of the answer- since it is only 2 digits long there is no need for carrying over.
- The answer is therefore 8235&36= 823,536.

Example 6: Extensions to larger numbers

$$289$$
$$x \quad 288$$

- The numbers are both below the nearest "100" (note that in this case the nearest 100 is 300) so we can apply this technique.

(Please note that both numbers have to be below the same 100- so if it was 289x388 the trick would not work, since one is below 300 whilst the other is below 400)

- The amounts by which the numbers are below the nearest 100 are: 11 and 12.
- Subtracting 11 from 288 or subtracting 12 from 289 gives 277.
- Since the nearest 100 which the two numbers are below is 300, we need to multiply the result by 3- so we calculate 277x3=831.

=> This is the left part of the answer. Link it to multiplex cinema.

- Now multiply the amount by which each number is below the nearest 100- i.e. multiply 11x12 =132; this is the right side of the answer, but since it is 3 digits long, we need to add any digits beyond the second digit to the left side of the answer. In the case of 132 we therefore split the number into 1&32; 1 is added to the left side of the answer and 32 remains the right side of the answer.
- So the left side of the answer becomes 831+1=832.
- The answer is therefore 832&32= 83,232.

Example 7: One below 100 one above 100

$$
\begin{array}{r}
104 \\
\times \quad 91 \\
\hline
\end{array}
$$

- Since both numbers are away from the same "100" we can use the technique.
- The amounts by which the numbers are away from the nearest 100 are: 4 and 9.
- **Adding** 4 to 91 or **Subtracting** 9 from 104 gives 95 – this is the left hand side of the answer => Link it to multiplex cinema.
- Now multiply the amount by which each number is over the nearest 100- i.e. multiply 4x9 =36.
- Multiply the left hand side of the solution (95) by 100 to get 9,500 from which you deduct the 36 obtained above.
- The answer is therefore 9500-36= 9,464.

Example 8: One below/one above – extended

$$814$$
$$x \quad 798$$

- Since both numbers are away from the same "100" (note in this case it is 800) we can use the technique.
- The amounts by which the numbers are away from the nearest 100 are: 14 and 2.
- **Adding** 14 to 798 or **Subtracting** 2 from 814 gives 812.
- Since the nearest 100 is actually 800, multiply the 812 by 8 to get 812x8= 6,496- this is the left hand side of the answer => Link it to multiplex cinema.
- Now multiply the amount by which each number is over the nearest 100- i.e. multiply 14x2 =28.
- Multiply the left hand side of the solution (6,496) by 100 to get 649,600 from which you deduct the 28 obtained above.
- The answer is therefore 649,600-24= 649,572.

Example 9: Thousands and onwards

$$1004$$
$$x \quad 1008$$

The technique is the same; the only difference is that the right hand side of the answer now has three digits instead of two.

- We now work with the nearest thousand rather than the nearest 100.
- So we get 1004+8=1012 => this is the left hand side of the answer.

- 4x8=32, since this is below 3 digits add a zero in the front to give 032=> this is the right hand side of the answer.
- Therefore the answer is 1012&032=1,012,032.

Another thousands-type example:

$$\begin{array}{r} 2015 \\ \times \quad 1988 \\ \hline \end{array}$$

- The nearest thousand is 2000.
- Add 15 to 1988 to get 2003, multiply by 2 to get 4006=> this is the left hand side.
- 15x12=180.
- Multiply 4006 by 1000 to 4,006,000 from this subtract 180 to get 4,005,820.

The same can be applied to millions and billions etc.

This trick is useful when the numbers are near 100 (or thousand or a million); however, when the numbers are too far from such a mark, the method can still be used but it does not offer a speedy solution- for such cases it is better to use the main multiplication technique.

Examples for which this method cannot be used:

- 219x912: in this case the hundreds which the numbers are over differ.
- 254x262: this is near the middle of the hundred and so does not offer a real shortcut.
- 1456x1589: using the thousand extension would not be useful as it would amount to calculating 456x589. Using the nearest 100 approach would not be useful either as it would require multiplying a 4 digit number by 15. The main multiplication method is more efficient for these cases.

Main multiplication method

The main method for multiplication should be used for all the cases that cannot be solved using the tricks presented above. The tricks are shortcuts that make the problem easier to solve, which is why they should always be used where possible- for everything else, the main method is the approach to take.

The main method is still a very quick approach to mental multiplication, but its real advantage is that it is simple and can be applied to any problem irrespective to the length of the numbers involved. As with all the techniques presented in this section, you can use the main multiplication method to calculate in your mind more than what is feasible on a standard calculator or excel application.

The procedure for this method is as follows:

1. If the problem is not written down, memorise the two numbers involved- you can use the link system.
2. If the numbers are not of the same length, add zeros to the left hand side of the shorter number until they are of the same length.
3. Begin multiplying the numbers across arches in the following sequence:
   a. Go from right to left:

abc x def

   b. As you go from right to left, increase the arches by one in each step- always working from outward to inward:

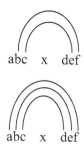

abc x def

c. In each step, you multiply the numbers on either end of the arches.

d. You then add up the results from each arch (it is recommended to add as you go along the arches, rather than multiply all arches and then add up- this way, there is no need to memorise the results of the multiplication but only the running total).

e. At every step, the rightmost digit of the sum from (d) is a digit of the solution and the rest of the digits are carried over.

f. You memorise using the loci system- at each step you peg the image for the digit from (e) to a point on your journey.

4. Once the outermost numbers have been reached, proceed by narrowing the arches in the opposite direction:

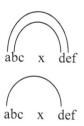

abc x def

5. Once the leftmost digits of each number have been reached, the computation is complete. You can then recover the

answer by stepping through your loci and recalling the numbers that you have pegged to objects along the way.

To remember the sequence of arches, simply think of a rainbow that is starting from the rightmost digit of the right number and going to the left, where it only reaches the rightmost digit of the left number. It then brings a friend on which it climbs and tries again, this time reaching the middle digit, whilst its friend start from the next digit on the right and lands one digit from the larger rainbow. It then continues, each rainbow bringing a friend until there are no more numbers on the left, at which point the rainbows leave one by one.

We proceed via examples in order to better illustrate the procedure; in the examples we will memorise the result using the following items which form part of a loci (the reader is advised to follow the exposition, but to then use their own loci with this method):

Items: Boat, pier, gate, car-park, ice-cream van, golf course, flower garden, statue, fountain.

Example 1: simple two digit problem: 12 x 34

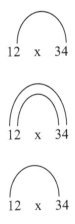

- We begin with the outmost arch between 2 and 4; we multiply the two numbers on either end of the arch to get 2x4=8. This is the first number (from the right) of the answer- we peg the image of this number, "Foe", (think of your worst enemy) to the first item on the journey (Boat).
- We move one step to the left and proceed to the next set of arches, between 1&4 and 2&3; we multiply the numbers on each end of the arch and add the results together- so we do: 1x4=4, 2x3=6 => 4+6=10. We take the rightmost digit of this result (0) and peg it to the next item on the journey (pier), we then take the remainder (1) and carry it forward.
- We move another step to the left and proceed with the next arch, between 1 and 3; we begin from the number we carried over from the previous step (1), we then add to it the multiple of the numbers at the end of the arch to get 1 + 1x3=1+3=4. Since there are no more arches, this is the final digit of the solution- we peg it to the third item on the journey (gate).
- To recall the solution, simply walk through the journey and recall the numbers (through their images) along the way: 408.

Example 2: three-digit problem: 345x857

345   x   857

345   x   857

- We begin with the first arch between 5 and 7; multiplying the two gives 35, five is therefore the first digit of the answer (peg it to the first item on the journey- boat) whilst 3 is carried over to the next stage.
- Proceeding to the next set of arches between 4&7 and 5&5; we take the remainder from the previous step (3) and add to it the results of multiplying the numbers at the end of the arches, so:

$$3+7x4+5x5=3+28+25=56$$

6 is the next digit of the answer; so peg it to the next item on the journey (pier); 5 is the remainder and it is carried over to the next step.
- Moving to the next set of arches between 3&7, 4&5 and 5&8; we take the remainder carried from the previous step (5) and add to it the results of multiplying the numbers at the end of each arch, so we get:

$$5+3x7+5x4+8x5= 5+21+20+40=86$$

(Note that you should multiply one arch at a time and keep a running total of the sum, rather than multiplying all

**arches and then add- this reduces the amount of data that
needs to be memorised and increases speed)**

6 is therefore the next digit of the answer so peg it to the next
item on the journey (gate), whilst 8 is the remainder and
should be carried to the next step.

- Proceed to the next set of arches, between 3&5 and 4&8; take
the remainder from the previous step (8) and add to it the
results of multiplying the numbers at the end of each arch, so:

$$8+3x5+8x4= 8+15+32= 55$$

The rightmost digit (5) is therefore the next digit of the
solution, so peg it to the next item on the journey (car-park);
the leftmost digit (also 5) is the remainder which is carried
over to the next step.

- Moving to the last arch, between 3 and 8; take the remainder
from the previous step (5) and add to it the result of
multiplying the two numbers at the ends of this arch, so:

$$5+3x8=5+24=29$$

- Therefore 29 is the final part of the solution, so peg this
number to the next item on the journey (ice-cream van). Notice
that the entire number is used here, instead of only the leftmost
digit, since there is no place to carry it to as we have reached
the end of the multiplication procedure.

Walk through your journey to recall the answer; notice that, if you
walk forwards in your journey, you will be recalling the answer from
right to left; whilst if you walk back through your journey, you recall
it from left to right. It is most often better to recall the number as you
memorised it, hence proceed by recalling travelling forward in your
journey (thus recalling the solution from right to left): 295,665.

238 | The Manual

Example 3: numbers of different sizes: 897x23

To perform this calculation we proceed exactly as before, but simply add zeros in front of the smaller number until it is of equal length to the larger number. So the problem becomes:

897x023

Proceeding as before, we get:

- $7 \times 3 = 21 \Rightarrow 1$ pegged to the 1st journey item, 2 carried over.
- $2 + 3 \times 9 + 2 \times 7 = 43 \Rightarrow 3$ pegged to the 2nd journey item, 4 carried over.
- $4 + 3 \times 8 + 2 \times 9 + 0 \times 7 = 46 \Rightarrow 6$ pegged to the 3rd journey item, 4 carried over.
- $4 + 2 \times 8 + 0 \times 9 = 20 \Rightarrow 0$ is pegged to the 4th journey item, 2 is carried over.
- $2 + 0 \times 8 = 2 \Rightarrow 2$ is pegged to the 5th journey item.
- The answer is therefore: 20,631.

Example 4: larger numbers

$$67,583 \times 88,504$$

The procedure is exactly the same, there are just more arches:

- $4\times3=12=>$ 2 pegged to the 1st journey item, 1 carried over.
- $1+4\times8+0\times3=33 =>$ 3 pegged to the 2nd journey item, 3 carried over.
- $3+4\times5+0\times8+5\times3=38 =>$ 8 pegged to the 3rd journey item, 3 carried over.
- $3+4\times7+0\times5+5\times8+8\times3=95 =>$ 5 is pegged to the 4th journey item, 9 is carried over.
- $9+4\times6+0\times7+5\times5+8\times8+8\times3=146 =>$ 6 is pegged to the 5th journey item, 14 is carried over.
- $14+0\times6+5\times7+8\times5+8\times8=153 =>$ 3 is pegged to the 6th journey item, 15 is carried over.
- $15+5\times6+8\times7+8\times5=141 =>$ 1 is pegged to the 7th journey item, 14 is carried over.
- $14+8\times6+8\times7=118 =>$ 8 is pegged to the 8th journey item, 11 is carried over.
- $11+8\times6=59 =>$ 59 is pegged to the 9th journey item.
- The answer is therefore: 5,981,365,832.

There is no limit; one can use this technique to multiply two 200 digit numbers if one really has the urge to.

The main key is to notice that memorisation only takes place at the end of each bunch of arches. There is no need to remember anything before that; simply take your remainder, add to it the result from the first arch, then add to that the result of the following arch and so on. There is no reason to first multiply all the arches and then add the results together- this would require memorising the result of each and would waste time (thus hindering speed). Simply add the results as you pass through the arches until you finish the bunch, then memorise the rightmost digit whilst carrying the remainder to the next step. To further enforce this point, in the last example above, the third step has: 3+4x5+0x8+5x3=38- since you are doing this mentally without writing it down, why bother memorising the results of the multiples (20, 0, 15)? Simply perform 3 + 4x5= 23, then 23+0x8=23, followed by 23+5x3=38. This way, the memorisation of interim steps is avoided and time is saved.

Finally, as illustrated for small numbers, when one number has more digits than the other, simply add zeros to the smaller number until they have an equal amount of digits- e.g. 9,837,672,123 x 5,546 should be solved as; 9,837,672,123 x 0,000,005,546. This is to ensure each arch has numbers on both ends.

Squaring

Squaring is simply a multiplication in which the two numbers multiplied are the same. Therefore, the approach to squaring is the same as that for multiplication with one small exception- numbers ending with 5 should be squared using a squaring trick; everything else is done exactly the same as for multiplication. The overall squaring procedure is as follows:

1. Does the number end with 5? If so, use the squaring trick.
2. If it does not end with a 5, is it near 100? If so use the multiplication tricks.
3. If it does not end with 5 nor is it near 100, simply use the main multiplication method.

Squaring trick

For numbers ending with 5 there is a simple trick that shortens the calculation. The procedure for this trick is as follows:

1. Split the number into two parts, the 5 on the right being one part and the rest of the number to its left is the other part.
2. Take the number on the left and multiply it with itself plus one- this gives the left part of the answer.
3. The right part of the answer is always 25.

Example 1: 25^2

- We begin by splitting the number into two portions, the 5 on the right and everything else on the left: 2&5.
- Take the number on the left (2) and add one to it: 2+1=3, and then multiply this result by the number on the left (2), so 2x3=6. This gives the left portion of the answer.
- The right portion of the answer is always 25.

- So the answer is 625.

Example 2: 85^2

- We begin by splitting the number into two portions, the 5 on the right and everything else on the left: 8&5.
- Take the number on the left (8) and add one to it: 8+1=9, and then multiply this result by the number on the left (8), so 8x9=72. This gives the left portion of the answer.
- The right portion of the answer is always 25.
- So the answer is 7,225.

Example 3: 115^2

- We begin by splitting the number into two portions, the 5 on the right and everything else on the left: 11&5.
- Take the number on the left (11) and add one to it: 11+1=12, and then multiply this result by the number on the left (11), so 12x11=132. This gives the left portion of the answer.
- The right portion of the answer is always 25.
- So the answer is 13,225.

Example 4: 985^2

- We begin by splitting the number into two portions, the 5 on the right and everything else on the left: 98&5.
- Take the number on the left (98) and add one to it: 98+1=99, and then multiply this result by the number on the left (98) - you can do it easily using the multiplication tricks introduced in the previous section- so 98x99=9,702. This gives the left portion of the answer.

- The right portion of the answer is always 25.
- So the answer is 970,225.

Example 5: 98^2

- This number does not end with 5 but it is near 100, so we use the multiplication tricks introduced earlier.
- 98 is 2 below 100; we therefore subtract 2 from 98 to get 96, this is the left portion of the answer.
- Take 2 and square it to get 4- this is the right portion of the answer.
- Therefore the answer is 9,604.

Example 6: 362^2

Since the number does not end with 5 nor is it near 100, we use the main multiplication method:

$$362 \times 362$$

- $2 \times 2 = 4 \Rightarrow 4$ pegged to the 1st journey item.
- $2 \times 6 + 6 \times 2 = 24 \Rightarrow 4$ pegged to the 2nd journey item, 2 carried over.
- $2 + 2 \times 3 + 6 \times 6 + 3 \times 2 = 50 \Rightarrow 0$ pegged to the 3rd journey item, 5 carried over.
- $5 + 6 \times 3 + 3 \times 6 = 41 \Rightarrow 1$ is pegged to the 4th journey item, 4 is carried over.
- $4 + 3 \times 3 = 13 \Rightarrow 13$ is pegged to the 5th journey item.
- The answer is therefore: 131,044.

Subtraction

Similar to addition, the method used for subtraction does not involve any tricks, but only a single simple approach that is applied to all problems. The procedure is as follows:

1. Is the number above larger than the one below? If not switch the positions and add a minus in front of the solution.
2. Solve from right to left.
3. Subtract the bottom number from the one above.
4. If it is not possible to subtract, simply add 10 to the number above- subtract the number below and carry forward a minus 1. Link the digit of the solution to the image of a submarine (subtract is shortened to sub and sub can mean submarine).
5. Step one digit to the left; if you carried forward a minus 1, simply subtract 1 from the number at the top of the column you are currently solving. If you did not carry a minus 1, continue the procedure as above. Link each image of the solution to the previous image.

Example 1:

$$
\begin{array}{r}
987 \\
-\ 325 \\
\hline
\end{array}
$$

- Begin at the rightmost column, subtract 5 from 7, so 7-5=2; this is the rightmost part of the answer. Link the image for 2 (knee) to a submarine. Perhaps a Knee is navigating a submarine.
- Step to the next column, subtract 2 from 8, so 8-2=6; this is the next digit of the solution, link the image for 6 (shoe) to the previous image (knee).

- Step to the next column, subtract 3 from 9, so 9-3=6; this is the next digit of the solution, link the image for 6 (shoe), to the previous image (also shoe) - perhaps a shoe it tying the laces of another shoe.
- Go through the images created, starting from submarine (since this is a subtraction problem) and you thus recall the solution from right to left. So the answer is: 662.

Note that, for long subtraction problems, it may be better to use a loci system in order to be able to easily remember repeated images. For example, if the solution was the following number: 54,555,535,535,553, some confusion may occur with the number 5 due to its repeated appearance. It is therefore easier to use the loci system for long problems. Alternatively, solving in pairs or triplets will also reduce the possibility for confusion; this is illustrated later in this section.

Example 2:

$$9571$$
$$- \quad 3628$$

- Begin with the rightmost digits; subtract 8 from 1, but since this is not possible (without going negative) simply add 10 to the top number (1), so 1+10=11; now subtract 8 from this number: 11-8=3. This is the rightmost part of the solution, link the image for 3 (MO) to submarine and carry a minus 1 to the next step.
- Since we carried a minus 1, simply subtract it from the top number (7), so 7-1=6; now subtract the bottom number from this "new top number", so 6-2=4. This is the next part of the solution- link the image for 4 (Row) to the previous image

(MO). Since we did not need to add a 10 here there is no need to carry anything.

- Step to the next column, subtract 6 from 5, but since this is not possible we need to add a 10 to the top number, so 5+10=15; now subtract 6 from this "new" top number: 15-6=9. This is the next part of the solution, link the image for 9 (Pie) to the previous image (Row) and carry a minus 1 to the next step.

- Step to the final column and subtract the carried minus 1 from the top number, so 9-1=8. Then subtract the bottom number from this new top number, so 8-3=5. This is the final part of the solution, simply link the image for 5 (Lee) to the previous image (Pie).

- Go through the images, starting from submarine, to retrieve the digits of the solution from right to left: 5,943.

Example 3: Working with doubles

With some practise, it is easier and more efficient to work with 2 digits at a time; this approach requires one to memorise less images and also flow through the problem much quicker. The procedure is exactly the same- the only difference is that we are considering two digits at a time instead of one.

$$
\begin{array}{r}
665802 \\
- \ 354978 \\
\hline
\end{array}
$$

- Begin with the rightmost double digits (02 at the top and 78 at the bottom); subtract 78 from 02, but since this is not possible proceed by adding a 100 to 02, so 100+02=10; now subtract 78 from this new number, so 102-78=24. This is the rightmost part of the solution, link the image for 24 (Honour) to submarine and carry a minus 1 to the next column.

- Move to the next two columns, subtract the carried minus 1 from the top number (58), so 58-1=57. Now subtract the bottom number (49) from this "new" number at the top, so 57-49=08. This is the next part of the solution, so link the image for 08 (Safe) to the previous image (Honour). **It is important to note that this portion of the solution is "08" rather than "8"; this is because we are working with 2 digits at a time and so the zero is significant.**
- Move to the final two columns, subtract 35 from 66; so 66-35=31; this is the last portion of the answer, link the image for 31 (Mad) to the previous image (Honour).
- Go through the images, starting from submarine, in order to retrieve the digits of the solution from right to left- so the answer is: 310,824.

A crucial note regarding the use of this system is in order: if the number at the top is smaller than the one at the bottom, then the answer would be negative. It is therefore important to first check whether the number at the top is indeed larger, if it is not, simply switch the positions of the two numbers and remember that the result is negative. Here is an example:

Example 4: Negative solutions

$$
\begin{array}{r}
414729 \\
- \quad 415691 \\
\hline
\end{array}
$$

The number above is smaller than the one below, so switch the numbers and remember to add a negative sign in front of the solution:

$$
\begin{array}{r}
415691 \\
- \quad 414729 \\
\hline
\end{array}
$$

- 91-29=62, link 62 to submarine.
- 56-47=09, link 09 to 62.
- 41-41=0.
- So the answer to the original problem is -962.

Division

Division involves a single approach that should be applied to all problems; the procedure is as follows:

1. Is the number being divided greater than the number dividing it (the divisor)?
   a. If yes, proceed with the procedure below.
   b. If not, for every time the number being divided needs to be multiplied by 10, move one decimal point in the solution.
2. Look at the number being divided from left to right, find the smallest portion that is greater than the divisor and then divide this portion (to the lowest integer) by the divisor. This gives you the first portion of the solution (from left to right)- peg it to the first item on your loci.
3. Multiply the result obtained in (2) above by the divisor and then subtract this amount from the portion of the number being divided that was used in (2) above. If after subtracting there is a remainder:
   a. Simply bring down the next digit in the number being divided and repeat the procedure above.
   b. If, after bringing down another digit, the remainder is still smaller than the divisor, simply add a zero to the solution and bring down another digit.
   c. If there are no more numbers to bring down, simply add a zero to the remainder and input a decimal place to the

solution- then repeat the procedure above. Add a big arrow to the image at this point in your loci to remind you where the decimal place resides.
4. Continue until there is no remainder or until the solution has been calculated to the desired decimal point.

The procedure appears long but, after some practise, it can be done quickly and comes very naturally. Division is an excellent all-round exercise since its procedure involves multiplication, division and subtraction.

Example 1: 789÷12

- First we look at the number being divided (789) and try to find the first portion (from left to right) that is greater than the divisor (12); since 7 is smaller than 12, the first portion that is greater than the divisor is 78.
- Divide this first portion (78) by 12 (note we try and find the lowest integer of the solution, not the precise result), so 78÷12=6.xxx, and thus the first part of the solution is 6. Peg the image for 6 (shoe) to the first item on your loci.
- Multiply 6 by the divisor, so 6x12=72, and subtract this number from the portion that was used to derive this part of the solution (i.e. 78), so 78-72=6. This is the remainder.
- Bring down the next digit and put it on the rightmost part of the remainder- so bring down the 9 (which is the next digit after the first portion (78) which we already used) and put it next to the 6 to give: 6&9=69.
- Now divide the next portion (69) by 12 to get: 69÷12=5.xxx- this is the next part of the solution. So peg the image for 5 (Lee) to the next item on your loci.

- Multiply 5 by the divisor, so 5x12=60. Now subtract this from the portion of the previous step (69), so 69-60=9. 9 is the new remainder.
- Since 9 is smaller than 12, we need to bring down another digit, but since there are no more digits in the number being divided, we bring down a zero and add a decimal place to solution. Peg the image of a gigantic arrow to the next item on your loci, to remind you where the decimal place of the solution is found.
- Bringing a zero gives us 9&0=90, so divide 90 by the divisor: 90÷12=7.xxx. This is the next digit of the solution- peg the image for 7 to the next item on the loci.
- Multiply 7x12=84 and subtract this from the number that was just divided in order to get the 7 (i.e. 90) - so 90-84=6. Since there are no more digits in the original number being divided and since we already added a decimal place, simply bring down a zero.
- So put the zero next to the remainder: 6&0=60.
- Next divide 60 by 12, so 60÷12=5; since the result is a pure integer (5), it is therefore the final digit of the solution- peg it to the next item on the loci.
- Now walk through the loci and recall the digits of the solution from left to right. The answer is therefore: 65.75.

For more complex problems, it is sometimes useful to link the image for the remainder to the image of a gigantic red rope; this is in order to be able to remember the remainder after the multiplication stage that takes place before it is used again. For example, in the calculation just performed, we had a remainder of 90 and then we had to multiply 7x12 to get the number which we needed to subtract from 90. We could have linked the image of 90 (Bus) to a gigantic red rope in order to remember that this is the remainder. We then would have proceeded to calculate 12x7=84 and we could have easily retrieved the remainder 90 (from which we need to subtract this 84) by thinking of a gigantic red rope. This avoids getting confused with the numbers during the calculation procedure and is only necessary when the remainder numbers are large.

<u>Example 2: 98,256÷564</u>

- 982÷564=1.xxx, peg 1 to the first item on your loci.
- 1x564=564, deduct this from 982, so 982-564=418.
- Bring down the next digit and put it on the right of 418: 418&5=4185; you can link the image for this number (perhaps RatVille) to a gigantic red rope to remember it for the next steps.
- 4185÷564=7.xxx, peg 7 to the next item on the loci.
- 7x564=3948, deduct this from 4185, so 4185-3948=237.
- Bring down the next digit, so 237&6=2376 (again you can link the image for this number to a gigantic red rope in order to remember it for the next steps)
- 2376÷564=4.xxx, peg 4 to the next item on the loci.
- 4x564= 2256, deduct this from 2376, so 2376-2256=120.
- Since no digits are left, bring down a zero, put a decimal point and peg an arrow to the next item on the loci.
- Take the zero you brought down and put it next to 120, so 120&0=1200 (link it to gigantic red rope).
- 1200÷564=2.xxx, peg 2 to the next item on the loci.
- 2x564=1128, deduct this from 1200, so 1200-1128= 72.
- Since no digits are left, bring down a zero; so we get 72&0=720.
- 720÷564=1.xxx, peg 1 to the next item on the loci.
- This loop can be continued until the desired decimal place. If we stopped at this stage and walked through the loci, it would gives the solution from left to right correct to 2 decimal places: 174.21.

Cube root

The method presented here is only applicable to whole roots; thus it will give a precise solution for the cube root of a number that has a root which is a whole number. However, it will only give an approximation if the number does not have a whole root. The procedure is very simple and is as follows:

1. Memorise the table of cubes for the numbers 0-9; it is provided below for your reference.
2. Split the number whose cube root you wish to extract into two parts; the rightmost part consists of the 3 rightmost digits, whilst the leftmost part consists of the rest of the digits of the number.
3. Find the number on the cube table of 0-9 that ends with the same digit as the rightmost portion derived in (2) above- this gives you the rightmost portion the solution.
4. Now look at the left portion of the number, find the number in the cube table of 0-9 which is closest from below; i.e. find the number that is smaller than or equal to the left portion of the number.

Table of cubes:

Number to be cubed	Cube
0	0
1	1
2	8
3	27
4	64
5	125
6	216
7	343
8	512
9	729

Example 1:

$$\sqrt[3]{17,576}$$

- We begin by splitting the number into two portion, 17&576.
- The right portion consists of 576, which ends with a 6; consulting the table of cubes (it is important to commit this table to memory so that it is not physically required when performing calculations) suggests that the cube of 6 (which is 216) ends with a 6; therefore, the right part of the solution is 6.
- The left portion of the problem consists of 17; consulting the table of cubes again, we find that the nearest cube that is smaller than 17 is the cube of 2 (i.e. 8); thus the left part of the solution is 2.
- The solution is therefore 2&6=26.

Example 2:

$$\sqrt[3]{912,673}$$

- We begin by splitting the number into two portion, 912&673.
- The right portion consists of 673, which ends with 3; consulting the table of cubes suggests that the cube of 7 (which is 343) ends with a 3; therefore, the right part of the solution is 7.
- The left portion of the problem consists of 912; consulting the table of cubes again, we find that the nearest cube that is smaller than 912 is the cube of 9 (i.e. 729). Thus, the left part of the solution is 9.
- The solution is therefore 9&7=97.

Example 3- non-whole roots:

$$\sqrt[3]{854,365}$$

- We begin by splitting the number into two portion, 854&365.
- The right portion consists of 365, which ends with 5; consulting the table of cubes suggests that the cube of 5 (which is 125) ends with a 5; therefore, the right part of the approximate solution is 5.
- The left portion of the problem consists of 854; consulting the table of cubes again, we find that the nearest cube that is smaller than 854 is the cube of 9 (i.e. 729). Thus, the left part of the approximate solution is 9.
- The approximate solution is therefore 9&5=95 [the precise solution is 94.8887].

It is important to re-iterate that this technique is precise only for whole roots; if the problem does not have a whole root, the solution which this technique provides is only an approximation.

For numbers larger than 1,000,000, it is necessary to have memorised the cubes of more than just 0-9. The rest of the procedure remains the same.

Higher roots

The technique introduced for the extraction of cube roots can be used for higher order odd roots. The main procedure remains the same; only the splitting out of the number changes and the tables for the higher roots also need to be memorised. As with cube roots, the technique only works for numbers that have whole roots; for numbers that do not have a whole root, the solution this technique provides is merely an approximation.

Procedure for higher order roots:

1. The technique only works for odd roots- so roots 3, 5, 7, 9, 11, etc...
2. Take the number whose root you are attempting to extract and split it into 2 portions. The right portion consists of the x rightmost digits of the number, where x is equal to the size of the root being extracted. E.g. x=3 for a cube root and x=5 for a quintic root.
3. The second portion of the number is everything to the left of the rightmost x digits.
4. Take the rightmost digit of the right portion and find the number on the corresponding table that ends with the same digit- this is the right part of the solution.
5. Take the left portion and find the nearest number on the table that is smaller than or equal to it- this is the left part of the solution.

Tables for higher order powers:

Number to be raised	Penteract (power of 5)	Hepteract (power of 7)	Enneract (power of 9)
0	0	0	0
1	1	1	1
2	32	128	512
3	243	2,187	19,683
4	1,024	16,384	262,144
5	3,125	78,125	1,953,125
6	7,776	279,936	10,077,696
7	16,807	823,543	40,353,607
8	32,768	2,097,152	134,217,728
9	59,049	4,782,969	387,420,489

Example 1:

$$\sqrt[5]{229{,}345{,}007}$$

- Since it is an extraction of root 5: we split the number into the rightmost 5 digits and everything else: 2293&45007.
- Starting with the right portion, 45007; using the table above (it should be committed to memory as was recommended for the cube table but only if this technique is of use to the reader) we find that the number to the power of 5 which gives a result that ends with a seven is 7- this is the right portion of the solution.
- Moving to the left portion of the number, we again consult the table to find the number whose Penteract (to the power of 5) is smaller than or equal to 2293- we find that this number is 4 (since 4 to the power of 5 is 1024 which is the nearest number that is smaller than or equal to 2293) - this is the left portion of the solution.
- The answer is therefore 47.

Example 2:

$$\sqrt[7]{17{,}565{,}568{,}854{,}912}$$

- Since it is an extraction of root 7: we split the number into the rightmost 7 digits and everything else: 1756556 & 8854912.
- Starting with the right portion, 8854912; using the table above (it should be committed to memory as was recommended for the cube table, but only if this technique is of use to the reader) we find that the number to the power of 7 which gives a result that ends with a two is 8- this is the right portion of the solution.
- Moving to the left portion of the number, we again consult the table to find the number whose Hepteract (to the power of 7) is smaller than or equal to 1756556- we find that this number is 7

(since 7 to the power of 7 is 823543 which is the nearest number that is smaller than or equal to 1756556) - this is the left portion of the solution.

- The answer is therefore 78.

Example 3:

$$\sqrt[9]{208,728,361,158,759}$$

- Since it is an extraction of root 9: we split the number into the rightmost 9 digits and everything else: 208728 & 361158759.
- Starting with the right portion, 361158759; using the table above (it should be committed to memory as was recommended for the cube table, but only if this technique is of use to the reader) we find that the number to the power of 9 which gives a result that ends with a nine is 9- this is the right portion of the solution.
- Moving to the left portion of the number, we again consult the table to find the number whose Enneract (to the power of 9) is smaller than or equal to 208728- we find that this number is 3 (since 3 to the power of 9 is 19683 which is the nearest number that is smaller than or equal to 208728) - this is the left portion of the solution.
- The answer is therefore 39.

Note- as with cube roots, this technique is only precise for numbers that have whole roots.

Square root

Similarly to cube and higher order odd roots, the method presented here is only applicable to whole roots. Therefore it will give a precise solution for the square root of a number that has a root which is a whole number; however, it will only give an approximation if the number does not have a whole root. The main difference of the approach for square roots is the need for an extra step, which is due to the repetition of some squares' rightmost digit. The procedure is as follows:

1. Split the number whose square root you wish to extract into two parts, the rightmost part consists of the 2 rightmost digits, whilst the leftmost part consists of the rest of the digits of the number.

2. Find the number whose square ends with the same digit as the rightmost portion derived in (1) above; for numbers ending with 5 or zero this is unique, but for the rest there are 2 possibilities. Thus, choose the lowest number whose square ends with the same number as the rightmost digit of the right portion of the problem- this gives you the <u>temporary</u> rightmost portion of the solution.

3. Now look at the left portion of the problem; find the number whose square is smaller than or equal to it- i.e. find the number that is smaller than or equal to the left portion of the number in the problem.

4. If the rightmost digit of the number in the problem is 5 or 0, then there is no need for an extra step; however, for all other numbers, take the left portion of the solution and add it to its square- if the number that results is greater than the left portion of the problem, then the temporary right portion was correct. If however, the result is lower than the left portion of the problem, then the right portion of the solution should be

swapped with the higher number that produces the same rightmost digit.

A few examples will more clearly demonstrate the procedure:

Example 1:

$$\sqrt{6,084}$$

- Split the number using the two rightmost digits, so we get 60&84.
- Find the lowest number whose square ends with 4- this is 2 which gives the temporary rightmost part of the solution.
- Find the lowest number whose square is smaller than or equal to 60- this is 7, which is the leftmost portion of the solution.
- Use the leftmost portion of the solution and add it to its square; so add 7 to 7 squared: 7+7x7=56; since 56 is below 60, we need to amend the rightmost part of the solution to the higher number, 8 (since the squares of 2 and 8 both end with 4 and since 8 is bigger, the answer is 8).
- The answer is therefore 78.

Example 2:

$$\sqrt{8,649}$$

- Split the number using the two rightmost digits, so we get 86&49.
- Find the lowest number whose square ends with 9- this is 3 which gives the temporary rightmost part of the solution.
- Find the lowest number whose square is smaller than or equal to 86, this is 9, which is the leftmost portion of the solution.

- Use the leftmost portion of the solution and add it to its square; so add 9 to 9 squared: 9+9x9=90; since 90 is above 86 (the leftmost part of the problem), we do not need to amend the rightmost part of the solution.
- The answer is therefore 93.

Example 3:

$$\sqrt{18,496}$$

- Split the number using the two rightmost digits, so we get 184&96.
- Find the lowest number whose square ends with 6- this is 4 which gives the temporary rightmost part of the solution.
- Find the lowest number whose square is smaller than or equal to 184; this is 13, which is the leftmost portion of the solution.
- Use the leftmost portion of the solution and add it to its square; so add 13 to 13 squared: 13+13x13=182; since 182 is below 184 we need to amend the rightmost part of the solution to the higher number, 6 (since the squares of 4 and 6 both end with 6 and since 6 is bigger, the answer is 6).
- The answer is therefore 136.

As with the odd roots, this method is only precise for numbers that have whole roots; for everything else, it would merely provide an approximation.

Decimals

The techniques above can be used on non-integers but require some modification; the simplest approach is to multiply the non-integer number by 10 until it becomes an integer and then reverse this in the answer. For example, multiplying 1.2x1.4 is the same as multiplying 14x12 and then dividing the answer by 100.

For addition and subtraction this is not necessary since we can simply add along and note when we reach the decimal point.

For division, it is the same as for multiplication but care needs to be taken when reversing; for example 124÷7.2 is the same as 124÷72 and then multiplying the answer by 10. This is because we only multiplied the divisor by 10- thus it needs to be reversed by multiplying the answer by 10. On the other hand, say we had 12.4÷7.2, it would then be the same as 124÷72 and there would be no need to reverse anything since the two multiplications by 10 cancel out.

For roots, it is necessary to multiply by a number that has a whole root; for example if it is a square root problem, we can multiply the problem by 100 and then divide the solution by 10. If it is a cube root, we can multiply the problem by a 1000 and then divide the solution by 10; for example the cube root of 474.552 is the same as the cube root of 474,552 divided by 10.

The key point is that any simplification introduced needs to be reversed in accordance with the operation being performed.

Training plan

The training plan simply involves practising the technique presented on a regular basis and incorporating them as much as possible into daily life. The following is the recommended approach that only requires 10mins a day, but in turn provides an excellent way to exercise the brain at the same time as mastering the techniques:

1. Use Microsoft Excel's RANDBETWEEN(,) function to generate random numbers of the length you wish to solve and produce one problem for each arithmetic function (i.e. one addition, one multiplication, one square etc...).
   a. Spend **10 minutes** every day solving the problems using the techniques above.
   b. As you become quicker, increase the size of the numbers.
   c. Recommendations for the beginning:
      i. Addition- Add 3 numbers consisting of 3 digits each.
      ii. Multiplication- Multiply two 3 digit numbers.
      iii. Subtraction- Subtract one 3 digit number from another.
      iv. Division- Divide a 3 digit number by a 1 or 2 digit number.
      v. Square- Square a 3 digit number.
      vi. Perform a cube root for a randomly generated number between 1-100 that has been cubed.
      vii. Perform a Penteract root for a randomly generated number between 1-100 that has been put to the power of 5.
2. Once the above becomes easy, move to 7-9 digits instead of 3 and also play with non-integers (e.g. 158.39 + 298.72).
3. Get used to adding your shopping items as you shop; see how close you are when you get to the till.
4. Perform all arithmetic in your mind as you encounter such problems in daily life; you can check your answers until you

gain confidence in your abilities- the main point is to develop the habit of solving in the mind without using calculators.

5. Measure your progress by tabulating how long it takes you to perform a calculation (keep the problem type the same, in order to make the measurement unbiased); for example: once a week, check how long it takes you to multiply two 3 digit numbers- tabulate your result and track your progress week by week.

Summary and Revision-Map

Key points

- Performing mental arithmetic trains the brain and can improve the practised skill as well as general mathematical abilities.
- The procedures for arithmetic involve several mental faculties (concentration, memory, problem solving and logic); thus it is an excellent all-round brain exercise.
- Addition, subtraction and division all apply a single procedure to all problems.
- Multiplication relies on tricks that facilitate the calculation of numbers near 100 whilst using a general method for everything else.
- Squaring uses a trick for numbers ending with 5 and uses the multiplication procedures for everything else.
- The root procedures rely on memorising key data components that speed up the solution for whole root problems.

Revision-Map

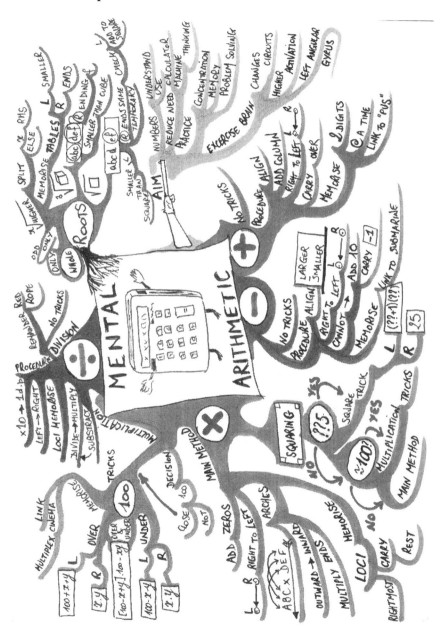

Afterword

This note on discipline was included for completeness; the systems presented in this manual do work, but they only work for those who persevere.

The author has decided that going into great details about discipline may miss the point; self-discipline is something that can be instilled only once a decision has been made in the person's mind. To arrive at that decision, a person has to toil through the pros and cons in terms of lifetime pain/pleasure combined with natural proclivities, all of which are usually specific to the individual and often quite personal. For this reason, the following three quotes are used to provide the reader with the food for thought necessary to arrive at a realisation about discipline and perseverance:

Discipline is the refining fire by which talent becomes ability.

Roy L. Smith

It was character that got us out of bed, commitment that moved us into action and discipline that enabled us to follow through.

Zig Ziglar

Success is not final, failure is not fatal: it is the courage to continue that counts.

Winston Churchill

Contact

For comments and enquiries about the book, as well as the private seminars/personal tuition provided by the author, please contact:

TheUSMmanual@gmail.com

You can also visit our website at:

www.UltimateStudyMethod.com

Reference and Extra reading

References of particular significance are starred (***); these are reserved for resources that, to the author's belief, provide a comprehensive yet practical coverage of a topic.

Concentration

Books:

1. *Accelerated Learning:* by Colin Rose.
2. *Cognitive psychology and its implication*: John Robert Anderson.
3. *** *Concentration*: by Mouni Sadhu.
4. *** *Jewish Meditation*: by Aryeh Kaplan.
5. *** *Kundalini Tantra:* by Swami Satyananda Saraswati.
6. *Meditation for Dummies:* by Stephan Bodian.
7. *Qigong Empowerment*: by Master Shou-Yu Liang and Wen-Ching Wu.
8. *Super-Learning 2000*: by Sheila Ostrander and Lynn Schroeder.
9. *Take Stress out of your life*: by Jay Winner M.D.
10. *** *The root of Chinese Qigong*: by Dr. Yang Jwing-Ming.
11. *** *The Silva Mind Control Method*: by José Silva and Philip Miele.

Scientific journals:

1. "Behavioural and ecological consequences of limited attention" Reuven Dukas.

2. "Cell phone-induced failures of visual attention during simulated driving." Strayer, David L.; Drews, Frank A.; Johnston, William A.

3. "Did Meditating Make Us Human?" Matt J. Rossano, *The Cambridge Archaeological Journal (2007), 17: 47-58.*

4. "Intensive meditation training leads to improvements in perceptual discrimination and sustained attention" Katherine A. MacLean, Emilio Ferrer, Stephen R. Aichele, David A. Bridwell, Anthony P. Zanesco, Tonya L. Jacobs, Brandon G. King, Erika L. Rosenberg, Baljinder K. Sahdra, Phillip R. Shaver, Alan Wallace, George R. Mangun & Clifford D. Saron.

5. "Meditation states and traits: EEG, ERP, and neuroimaging studies" Cahn BR, Polich J.

6. "The neural basis of the complex mental task of meditation: neurotransmitter and neurochemical considerations" Newberg AB, Iversen J.

Memory

Books:

1. *How to develop a super power memory*: by Harry Lorayne.
2. *Maximize your memory*: by Ramón Campayo.
3. ***Mega Memory: by Kevin Trudeau.
4. *Page-a-minute memory book*: by Harry Lorayne.
5. ****Super memory - super student*: by Harry Lorayne.
6. *The memory book:* by Harry Lorayne and Jerry Lucas.
7. *Tricks of the mind*: by Derren Brown.
8. *Use your perfect memory*: by Tony Buzan.

Scientific journals:

1. "The Magical Number Seven, Plus or Minus Two: Some Limits on our Capacity for Processing Information." Miller, G.A. (1956), *Psychological Review*, 63, 81-97.
2. "The influence of acoustic and semantic similarity on long-term memory for word sequences" Baddeley, A. D. (1966), Quart. J. Exp. Psychol 18 (4): 302–9.
3. "Effects of a 14-day healthy longevity lifestyle program on cognition and brain function", Small GW, Silverman DH, Siddarth P, Ercoli LM, Miller KJ, Lavretsky H, Wright BC, Bookheimer SY, Barrio JR, Phelps ME (June 2006), *The American Journal of Geriatric Psychiatry : Official Journal of the American Association for Geriatric Psychiatry* 14 (6): 538–45.
4. "Memory: A Contribution to Experimental Psychology", Ebbinghaus (1885/1913).

Speed Reading

Books:

1. ***Breakthrough rapid reading:* by Peter Kump.
2. *Méthode de Lecture rapide*: by François Richaudeau [in French].
3. ***Photoreading*: by Paul R. Scheele, M.A.
4. *Rapid Reading*: by Geoffrey A. Dudley.
5. *Super Reading Secrets*: by Howard Stephen Berg.
6. *The complete idiot's guide to speed reading*: by Abby Marks Beale with Pam Mullan.
7. *The Evelyn wood 7-Day speed reading & learning program*: by Stanley D. Frank, Ed.D.
8. *The Speed reading book*: by Tony Buzan.
9. *Triple your reading speed*: by Wade E. Cutler.

Scientific journals:

1. "An analysis of the rapid reading controversy" Brown, B., D. Inouye, K. Barrus, and D. Hansen. 1981. *The social psychology of reading: Language and literacy*, Vol. 1. ed J. Edwards. Silver Spring, MA: Institute of Modern Languages.
2. "Preliminary analysis of Photoreading" McNamara D.S, Old Dominion University [prepared for NASA].
3. "Rate and reading dynamics reconsidered" Cranney, A., B. Brown, D. Hansen, and D. Inouye. 1982. *Journal of Reading*, 25, pp. 526–533.

Note Taking

Books:

1. *Effective notetaking:* by Fiona McPherson.
2. *Mind Maps at Work: How to Be the Best at Your Job and Still Have Time to Play*: by Tony Buzan.
3. *Note-Taking Made Easy*: by Judi Kesselman-Turkel and Franklynn Peterson.
4. ****The mind map book*: by Tony and Barry Buzan.
5. *Use Both Sides of Your Brain: New Mind-Mapping Techniques*: by Tony Buzan.

Rapid Arithmetic

Books:

1. *Math Magic*: by Scott Flansburg with Victoria Hay Ph.D.
2. *More Rapid Math Tricks and Tips*: by Edward H. Julius.
3. *Speed Mathematics*: by Bill Handley.
4. *** *The Trachtenberg speed system of basic mathematics*: translated and adapted by Ann Cutler and Rudolph McShane.

Scientific journals:

1. "Dissociating neural correlates of cognitive components in mental calculation." Gruber O, Indefrey P, Steinmetz H, Kleinschmidt A.
2. "Effects of long-term practice and task complexity on brain activities when performing abacus-based mental calculations: a PET study." Wu TH Chen CL Huang YH Liu RS Hsieh JC Lee JJ.
3. "Individual differences in mathematical competence predict parietal brain activation during mental calculation" RH Grabner, D Ansari, G Reishofer, E Stern, *NeuroImage* Volume 38, Issue 2, 1 November 2007, Pages 346-356.
4. "Learning by strategies and learning by drill—evidence from an fMRI study" M. Delazera, , , A. Ischebeckb, F. Domahsc, L. Zamariana, F. Koppelstaetterd, C.M. Siedentopfd, L. Kaufmanne, T. Benkea and S. Felberd, *NeuroImage* Volume 25, Issue 3, 15 April 2005, Pages 838-849.
5. "Learning complex arithmetic—an fMRI study" M. Delazer a, , , F. Domahs a, L. Bartha a, C. Brenneis a, A. Lochy b, T. Trieb c and T. Benke a, *Cognitive Brain Research*, Volume 18, Issue 1, December 2003, Pages 76-88.

Index